Inside Jamaican Schools

University of the West Indies Press
1A Aqueduct Flats   Mona
Kingston 7   Jamaica

07   5 4

CATALOGUING IN PUBLICATION DATA

Evans, Hyacinth.
    Inside Jamaican schools / Hyacinth Evans

    p. cm.
    Includes bibliographical references and index.
    ISBN: 976-640-097-0
    1. Schools – Jamaica. 2. Teaching – Jamaica. 3. Curriculum
    evaluation – Jamaica. 4. Education, secondary – Jamaica.
    I. Title.

    LC210.8.J3E82 2001   370.7292

    Book design by Cecille Maye-Hemmings
    Cover design by Errol Stennett

PRINTED BY PHOENIX PRINTERY LTD.

Inside Jamaican Schools

Hyacinth Evans

University of the West Indies Press
Barbados • Jamaica • Trinidad and Tobago

For Jessica

Contents

Preface   viii

Acknowledgments   xii

Abbreviations   xiii

Chapter 1   SCHOOLS AND SCHOOLING   1

Chapter 2   THEORETICAL PERSPECTIVES: APPROACHES TO UNDERSTANDING AND STUDYING SCHOOLS   16

Chapter 3   INSIDE CLASSROOMS: TEACHERS, STUDENTS AND AUTHORITY   30

Chapter 4   THE CURRICULUM AND TEACHING: WHAT SCHOOLS AND CLASSROOMS TEACH AND HOW IT IS TAUGHT   67

Chapter 5   STREAMING AND ITS EFFECTS ON STUDENTS   90

Chapter 6   LANGUAGE IN THE CLASSROOM   105

Chapter 7   GENDER IN THE SCHOOL SETTING   136

Chapter 8   TOWARD BETTER SCHOOLS FOR ALL   143

Notes   151

References   156

Index   161

Preface

This book is about what happens in schools and classrooms. It focuses on the experiences of students and teachers, and draws on research that I have conducted, as well as on research carried out by some of my students in Jamaica over the past twelve years. The research is distinctive in that it used qualitative methods of data collection. This method, also known as ethnography, relies on participant observation and interviewing, and aims at understanding peoples' lives, perspectives, and ways of thinking. This approach to studying schools provides an up-close view of what takes place in schools and gives a picture of the social reality of schools – the experiences and perspectives of teachers, students, principals, and parents.

One of the purposes of this book is to provide this up-close view of schools and classrooms – to describe in an ethnographic way the experiences of those who work and learn in schools, and to examine the ways in which young people are shaped and identities formed in face-to-face interaction. These descriptions also present the ways in which society's tensions are played out in these settings. Schools are institutions created by the society; they have a formative influence on and help to shape that society. In a postcolonial society, one has to be mindful of this influence and constantly and vigilantly monitor received values, beliefs, and practices in schools.

A second purpose is to show the ways in which educational theories can be used to understand what happens in schools. A theory or theoretical framework is simply a way of looking at, or interpreting, social situations or events, a view which is quite different from that seen when other theoretical frameworks are used. Theoretical frameworks also provide a set of ideas or concepts for describing what exists and posits certain relationships among the elements in question. Educational theories attempt to explain educational outcomes and especially differences in outcomes based on social class, race or colour, and gender.

A third aim of the book is to show through the research reported, the ways in which specific events in schools exemplify educational theories. The extracts from the research illustrate the ways in which individual thought and action are linked and how each is influenced by the structure or the institutional context. According to Giddens (1979: 49), an important task in social theory is that of connecting human action with structural explanation. This is also an important aim of research in general, and of this book. The research to be discussed in this book presents students' "subjectivity" – their viewpoints, their assessments of others' actions, the ways in which students actually confront schooling. The book also discusses the ways in which aspects of the school environment and teacher discourse – i.e., aspects of structure – influence this subjectivity and their engagement in school. By providing these ethnographic descriptions of events in schools, and linking what happens to institutional and structural features, I hope that I take a critical stance in looking at education and schooling in Jamaica. I try to examine the links between individual action, local school cultural practices, and the wider community. In the end, my aim is not simply to portray the actual, but to consider the possible.

My focus in the volume is on some types of schools and some groups of students. The book begins with a description of the different types of schools in Jamaica, but focuses on the ones that are disadvantaged or are attended by students from the poorer classes. It describes in more detail these schools and these students and examines the ways in which their experiences are influenced by economic, social, and cultural factors. The book falls within the tradition of sociological ethnography in education, using research data from Jamaican schools. It attempts to describe schools and classrooms and events that occur within them, while at the same time presenting a theoretical sociological analysis of those events. As such, it fills a need for a book on education that describes and investigates specific aspects of schools and analyses these events from a theoretical sociological perspective. Such a book does not now exist.

Overview of the Book

The first chapter on education and schooling examines the school as a social institution that exists for specific aims and functions, not all of which are educational. It also outlines the historical legacy of education in Jamaica, and describes the diversity of schools. The second chapter discusses alternative theoretical frameworks for understanding schools and schooling and the research methods associated with each perspective. The third chapter looks at life inside the classroom and examines conceptually the nature of the relationship between teachers and students and in particular, the delicate nature of teacher authority. It makes clear that teacher authority has to be earned by teachers and cannot be arbitrary. In presenting the perspective of teachers, extracts from a research by Frances

Coke (1991) on high school teachers illustrate the ways in which teacher commitment is formed and nurtured in the Jamaican high school. It also discusses the many reasons why these teachers who taught in the 1980s lost their commitment to teaching and decided to switch careers. In so doing, the research touches on some of the sources of teacher satisfaction. In discussing the issue of teacher authority, the chapter draws on research conducted by Pauline Brown (1997) and illustrates the ways in which the teacher's authority is maintained, nurtured or eroded especially in a low stream class. This research has something important to say about learning (or failure to learn), about student/teacher interaction and its effects, and the social construction of student interest and attention, or of disruptiveness and apathy.

Chapter 4 examines the curriculum and the processes of teaching and learning in the all-age schools where materials and resources are limited. It presents two extracts from research that I conducted in 1988. The first extract describes the teaching of one teacher who had the characteristics and attitudes of an effective teacher and who, despite the constrained circumstances under which she worked, was able to show caring and encouragement to her students. The second extract describes a model of teaching so often seen in these schools where there is little learning or interest in learning, and where the emphasis is on the teacher writing words on a chalkboard and students copying them in their exercise books. These two extracts illustrate the ways in which learning (and not learning) are socially constructed, but heavily influenced by material resources as well as teacher commitment.

Chapter 5 discusses the effects of streaming on students and presents an extract from research by Yusuf-Khalil (1993) which contrasts the experiences of students placed in the high and low streams in two all-age schools and one primary school. She found that placement in stream correlated with the socioeconomic status, i.e. students who were from the middle classes were placed in the high stream, while children of labourers were usually placed in the low stream. Corporal punishment, a normal part of schooling in many Jamaican schools, was particularly excessive in the low stream, as was verbal abuse of students. Yusuf-Khalil found that students in the low stream demonstrated low self-esteem, because they evaluated themselves on the basis of teachers' treatment of them as well as on the basis of the stream in which they were placed.

Chapter 6 discusses attitudes to the Creole language in the society and in the educational system. It reports on an experiment in the use of alternative teaching and learning strategies and materials in the teaching of Standard Jamaican English to Grade 7 students whose first language was Creole. It describes the actual curriculum in use in the classroom, the specific activities required by the new methods, the teaching/learning materials employed, and the ways in which both students and teachers responded to the innovation. In addition, it analyses some of the errors that Creole- speaking students made as they attempted to use Standard Jamaican English.

Chapter 7 discusses gender in the Jamaican classroom. It reports some aspects of the research carried out by Yusuf-Khalil and illustrates the gender differences in the treatment of low stream boys and girls as well as some of the ways in which masculinity and femininity can be constructed in the school environment. Chapter 8, "Toward Better Schools for All", contrasts the vision of schools – what schools can be – with the stark realities of schooling and the challenges that they have to face in the early years of the twenty-first century. It ends with some possible directions for the immediate future.

As the objectives of the book indicate, I have tried to combine descriptions of schools with theoretical analyses of what happens in them. The result can be interpreted as a critique of schools. I have tried to avoid being overly critical of schools by emphasizing the constraints under which they and especially teachers work, the challenges of teaching and of teacher/student interactions. I hope that I have succeeded in creating a balance. It is my hope that this book will be of interest to an audience that is seriously interested in knowing more about schools, and how we can improve them. The book should also be of interest to students of education, in particular graduate students who conduct research, and use theoretical perspectives to analyse their findings. The book does not provide any prescriptions for change, though the last chapter reminds us of the mission of schools and a vision for the future.

Acknowledgments

Many individuals contributed to the preparation of this book. I should like to thank my former students – Miss Pauline Brown, Mrs Frances Coke, and Mrs Yasmeen Yusuf-Khalil – for allowing me to use extracts from the research that they carried out as requirements for courses on Qualitative Research Methods and Inside Classrooms. I should also like to thank the many other students on these courses whose research opened my eyes to many aspects of life in schools. My thanks also to the Rotary Club of Kingston and in particular its chairman in 1998 who gave me permission to include the research on "Operation English" in this book. My very special thanks to the two reviewers – Dr Anne Hickling-Hudson and Dr Ruby King – for their reading of the initial manuscript and their very helpful comments which served to significantly improve its quality.

Abbreviations

CXC	Caribbean Examinations Council
GCE	General Certificate of Education
JC	Jamaican Creole
JHSC	Jamaica High School Certificate
JUT	Jamaica Union of Teachers
MOEC	Ministry of Education and Culture
NVQJ	National Vocational Qualification of Jamaica
PEIP	Primary Education Improvement Project
ROSE	Reform of Secondary Education
SJE	Standard Jamaican English
SSC	Secondary School Certificate
UCLA	University of California, Los Angeles
WICP	Women in the Caribbean Project

1

Schools and Schooling

Schools and classrooms are familiar places. Most of us have attended some type of school and have images in our minds of what they are or represent. We may think of their outward appearance – the buildings, the classrooms, the principal's office, the playground. Or we may think of the ceremonies, the visits, and our experiences as student or parent. We may recall happy events or we may have painful memories. We all have personal connections to schools and classrooms. Schools and what happens in them are important to us not only because of these personal connections, but because they are institutions which help to create a society on which the future of our nation depends. They are social institutions to which society has given a particular mission to develop the young in worthwhile ways – to pass on knowledge and values, and to develop capacities, skills, and dispositions. This is education and it is what schools do everywhere, though the form of that education differs from society to society and even within a particular society.

When we think about our schools, we have specific images of these places and of what occurs in them. We may remember the ones we attended or the ones attended by our children. We can be critical of what happens in schools, for we hold up these events against certain standards. We may decry the types of behaviour which now appear commonplace in schools, or raise eyebrows at the number of passes in the Caribbean Examinations Council (CXC) examination. We may feel that teachers' expectations for students are too high or too low. We have many expectations for schools, not all of which can be fulfilled. Those who work in schools also have aims and visions that guide their work. But their achievements are not always close to those aims and visions. Teachers, students, principals, and parents – those who spend time in schools – are mindful of the tension which separates what occurs in schools from what is expected, and what ought to be. Society's expectations are many. We want schools to overcome problems of illiteracy, to overcome problems of violence, to prepare good citizens, to teach young people manners and respect for the elderly. We want our teachers to be models of proper behaviour, to teach our children well, and to help them to be successful in school. We expect that the schools will provide our children with upward social mobility.

From the beginning of our history, education was seen as the means for escaping the harsh physical conditions of working the soil with little or no return for the effort. This is what one observer had to say of the efforts to obtain an education by the society which had just been made free:

> The public enthusiasm on behalf of the freed slaves found expression in large subscriptions for educational purposes to the various religious bodies. (After the schools were established) schools all over the island filled with the most eager and docile of pupils (Great Britain, 1901: 579).

But this writer continued, "the schools established were for the most part of very inferior description" and teaching was "almost entirely by rote" or "sound without sense". Soon after these schools were established, many of these students no longer flocked to these classrooms, no doubt because of a curriculum irrelevant to their lives and out of step with their dreams and because the teaching methods were lacking in interest and challenge. The elementary school to which the writer referred was established primarily for the purpose of maintaining Jamaica's stratified social structure and of socializing students to take their place in that structure through "habit, training, doctrine and discipline – not book learning" (Turner, 1987: 60). The aims of education, the resources made available and the curriculum have changed over the years, but many of Jamaica's schools still reflect this history.

While some in our society have become very critical of our schools and our teachers, we continue to have faith in schools as a means for obtaining certification, employment, and upward social mobility. The state

2

expects that education will contribute to national development and the development of a learning society. Our criticism of schools is much sharper because of the exalted goals we have for them. It is true that historically, education has provided some degree of upward social mobility for many Jamaicans, though it has done so to a lesser extent for some groups than for others. Social mobility for many Jamaicans has been most marked during the years after the Second World War (Gordon, 1987). During these years, an expansion in the economy led to a change in the composition of the labour force. An urban managerial, professional, and clerical middle class developed, as did an urban working class of factory and service workers. Gordon (1987), in his study of inter-generational mobility during these years, provides data to show that most of the workers in these new sectors came from homes of small farmers and peasants. Thus, a social space was created by the economic expansion and this was filled by many Jamaicans from a poor rural background.

Education – or at least some years of high schooling – was an important factor in this social mobility. At the same time, however, a large section of the Jamaican population – agricultural labourers, unskilled manual labourers, and service workers – have experienced very little mobility. According to Gordon, we have seen during the postwar period, "the paradox of large-scale social mobility coexisting side by side with gross and perhaps even widening inequalities of opportunity between the minority at the top and the majority at the bottom of the social order" (p. 2). Those at the bottom of the social order are the groups who have not received the benefits of education and have consequently not enjoyed any social mobility. The child of the agricultural or unskilled labourer will, in all likelihood, become an agricultural or unskilled labourer. This is the case despite an expansion of educational offerings over the years. The paradox to which Gordon referred may be explained in part by the differences in the quality and quantity of provisions for schooling made available to the children of those at the top and of those at the bottom of this order. It may also be explained by the differences in the processes of schooling in these schools – the expectations, and the interactions between students and teachers.

Although access to secondary education has improved for the children of the poor, they are still underrepresented at this level of education. For example, in 1997–98, only 65.2 percent of the fifteen- to sixteen-year-olds in the poorest consumption group (the lowest quintile) were enrolled in secondary education compared with 94.3 percent of the wealthiest

3

group (the highest quintile). Access to the upper levels of secondary education is more limited, as there are places for only 46 percent of the age cohort. But poor students are even less represented at this level; only 17.8 percent of the seventeen- to nineteen-year-olds in the poorest consumption group were enrolled in 1997–98, compared with 62.7 percent of the wealthiest group (Planning Institute of Jamaica, 1998). There are also variations in access to the different types of secondary schools for different social classes.[1] Children of poor parents are overrepresented in schools that are considered of lesser quality – the all-age school and the primary and junior high schools. These schools terminate at Grade 9 with few or no opportunities for further education.

What Schools Are For

Like the public which holds up schools to careful scrutiny against society's standards and expectations, those who study schools have a dual perspective on schools and what happens in them. They are mindful of what schools ought to do, while being aware of what they do or are able to do. Schools exist for the purpose of educating children, and the concept of education points to certain end points or achievements. But the processes and activities of education must be judged by certain criteria (Peters, 1967). These end points or achievements are defined in different ways by different societies, and are subject to debate. Dewey's (1916) view of this end point is at once simple and complex. He asserts that "in dealing with the young . . . our chief business with them is to enable them to share in a common life" (p. 7). Sharing in a common life implies many things, including sharing common values, and learning to live and commune with others in respectful ways. It may also mean having the skills to make a living, to raise a family, and to make a contribution to society. The school's mission may be interpreted narrowly or broadly. If, in addition, we accept, as Dewey does, that one important aim of education in a democracy is to prepare individuals for democracy (1916: iii), then the school not only has to teach about democracy but also to practise it as well as to provide activities which will allow students to experience and reflect on democratic behaviour and democratic ideals.

Knowledge and cognitive skills are obviously important educational goals. Emotional maturity, self-assurance, discipline, and social skills also help in forming the ability to share in this common life. The ideas of philosophers are helpful in formulating our goals for education. Peters (1967), for example, believes that to be educated, one's way of looking at things must be transformed in some way. Dewey believes that as a result of education, we should be able to reorganize or take a fresh look at our experience, and that an educational activity should influence later experience (Dewey, 1916: 33). Martin (1985) argues that education should serve to make the person more accepting and appreciative of his or her culture and not, as often happens, to become alienated from it. Education should also make one more able to understand feelings and emotions and to unite feelings and emotions with action. The definition of these end points – what schools should do for students – is an issue which engages many societies. In Jamaica, however, public debate about such issues – what these end points should be – rarely occurs. What we do have are policy statements about the goals of education formulated by government officials. For the primary level of education, the policy document states that "the child completing primary school should be functionally literate and numerate, demonstrating a positive self-concept and a willingness to take responsibility for his/her learning. He/she should be culturally, aesthetically and spiritually aware and be guided by a commitment to social and moral principles" (Ministry of Education and Culture [MOEC], 1999a: vii). In another document, it is stated that by Grade 6, students should have achieved "literacy and numeracy by global standards, competence in the prerequisite knowledge and skills required to gain access to secondary education and should possess a caring attitude towards self, others, and things" (MOEC, 1991: 10). Similar goals are not articulated for the secondary level, perhaps because of the diversity of the offerings at that level. In the recent Green Paper on Education (MOEC, 1999a), the Ministry aims to "provide quality education for all", to "devise and support initiatives striving towards literacy for all" and to promote "cultural development, awareness and self-esteem for individuals, communities and the nation" (p. 6). Although these are stated as objectives in the Green Paper, they are vague enough to be interpreted in many ways. Indeed, this Green Paper with its emphasis on explaining cost-sharing and partnership arrangements, sidesteps the responsibility of articulating desirable end points or criteria for educational processes at the school level. Such details, one concludes, are to be developed by the local school.

Educational goals may not always reflect the aspirations of individuals and families who may have varying expectations for education. And it is likely that different groups of parents have different expectations for their

5

schools. Most, however, would expect the school to instil some kind of discipline in their children. In a study of all-age schools, Evans (1988) found that parents of all-age school students had few expectations for the school other than to prepare their children to pass the selection examinations for secondary school, i.e., the Common Entrance Examination, the Technical Examination, and the Grade Nine Achievement Test. At the same time, these parents — mostly rural folk engaged in small farming or higglering — were quite aware of the unlikelihood of their children gaining a place in a secondary school. So additionally, they wanted the all-age school to give their children skills for earning a living. Parents in other types of schools and from a different social class background have different expectations, and may be less likely to accept limited opportunities for their children.

There is also little consensus on the processes of education or teaching that would allow the school to realize these goals. The conventional view of teaching in many parts of the world is the delivery of content to students. It is believed that what the teacher needs most of all is a thorough knowledge of content and some classroom experience (Goodlad, 1984; Stones, 1994). And even though various educational theories have emphasized the importance of such matters as student interests, child centredness, and democratic processes, these ideas have not penetrated conventional practice at the secondary level. Recently, however, school reform efforts worldwide have begun to focus on the quality of learning experiences — the teaching methods or teaching style of the teacher, and the relationship between the teacher and the student as a means of improving the quality of education. These approaches to teaching and learning require the teacher and the student to play new and different roles. These reforms are evident in the Reform of Secondary Education (ROSE) and the Primary Education Improvement Project (PEIP) now being implemented in Jamaica.[2]

When we think of these end results of education and schooling — success in examinations, skills and knowledge required for citizenship and gainful employment — we are thinking of the instrumental ends of education and schooling. But schooling is also a social activity engaged in by students from various backgrounds and with a variety of interests. Students interact with each other and, in so doing, produce or create a culture that is centred on the peer group. It is perhaps safer to say that different cultures are created since student groups are created around interests and common preferences. In these friendship groups, students discuss matters of importance to them: friends and friendship, teachers, parents, boys or

6

girls, sex, and their hopes for the future. They may engage in silly games, ridicule teachers or other students to get a laugh, break the boredom of schooling, and simply pass the time of day. It is through these friendship groups that students' identity is socially constructed. This is especially critical for the adolescent who is going through a period of transition and transformation. It is in these peer or friendship groups that students — particularly adolescents — develop knowledge of self, social skills, and social networks.

This social informal side of school can work in concert with or against the official goals of the school. Some activities in which students learn these social skills are organized by the school. For example, some schools organize after-school social and cultural activities that can play a very important role in the personal and social development of students. In this way, students can, through the auspices of the school, create or produce a culture which forms the context for their personal and social development. When asked to reflect on the value of their education, Caribbean women have emphasized the socializing aspects as the greatest benefits — more important than the cognitive and practical skills which would have prepared them for the job market (McKenzie, 1986). And secondary school graduates value the friendship networks formed during those critical formative years. At the same time, McKenzie (1986: 96) concluded that for the women interviewed in the Women in the Caribbean Project (WICP), education had served to socialize them into passivity and acceptance of a conventional female role.

Students expect fair and equal treatment from adults, but do not always receive this from their teachers. An unavoidable feature of school life is the difference in age and authority between teachers and students — a difference that sometimes leads to claims on the part of students of unfair treatment and misuse of authority. Connell et al. (1982) found in their study of Australian schools that this was a widespread criticism of schools — "arbitrary authority, poor teaching, inconsistent discipline, favouritism, lack of respect for kids" (p. 85). Some students resist such teacher behaviours, and this resistance may be expressed in simple ways such as silence when they are expected to speak; or they may do so in more confrontational ways. This resistance sometimes becomes a social activity, one that depends on a good deal of support and encouragement from peers. Indeed, Connell et al. (1982) argue that for some students, resistance to school practices is a "consequence even in some respects, a form of class struggle" (p. 85). Increasingly, students are becoming more ready to openly resist teachers' unfair treatment or practices.

7

Many students and the groups to which they belong are able to establish a good relationship with teachers and other adults in the school. But this is not the case with all students. Some students may form groups or organize activities that are in opposition to the goals of the school. Tensions may also arise among groups of students within the school. Some student groups may create their own patterns of behaviour which are oppositional to school values and requirements, but which nevertheless afford them some solidarity. Some students bring to the school their own ideology, cultural forms, values and expectations that may differ according to class or ethnic group. This makes students respond to school practices, rules and requirements in ways counter to what the school expects. This is what Solomon (1988, 1992) found in the case of Caribbean male students in Toronto. These Caribbean youth created their own cultural forms within the school in their attempt to develop some group solidarity and identity, as well as to create a zone of protection in what they saw as a hostile school environment. What is also apparent is that these students' practices – a form of cultural production within the school – sometimes work to affect student engagement in classrooms and in learning activities. In extreme cases, students may engage in actions which pit them (and their community's values) against those of the school. Such actions challenge the role and the authority of the school (and hence of the society which gives the school its legitimacy). This expression of the social informal side of schooling and the tensions created with the official formal level of schooling highlight the social tensions that exist in the wider society.

When we look outside of the school rather than focus on what happens inside, we can regard education and schooling as a phase in the human life course. Education and schooling are a critical phase in the transition from childhood or youth to adulthood. The way we negotiate the transition is critical for later adulthood, not only in the skills and dispositions learned, but also in the personality formed, the social networks created and the sense of empowerment, and the sense of one's place in the society that one develops. The school is the major social institution that prepares youth for the adult world and particularly for the job market. Because of this common school experience that all the young in most societies undergo, schooling is seen as having the potential for integrating and unifying elements of the society through exposure to a common curriculum and to common ideas and ideals. Dewey (1916) envisioned the school as the site for the preparation for democracy. But the experience of schooling and the socialization received often differ according to one's race, class, and gender. Two students can attend the same school and be in the same class with the same teacher and yet have contrasting experiences and memories of those years. And when they attend different types of schools, the possibility of having different socialization experiences is even greater. It is increasingly evident that students also have differential access to knowledge even within the same school because of organizational features of school such as streaming. Thus, although it is often argued that schooling can be an integrative unifying force, the reality is often just the opposite.

When schooling is placed in the context of the human life cycle, normative assumptions are usually made about that life course. It is assumed that the student is dependent on parents who are supportive, and that the stages of the life course are independent of each other. So one is expected to move from being a student (where one lives at home in a state of dependency) to employment, living on one's own, marriage and then parenthood (Pallas, 1993). Variations in this sequence can have serious consequences on achievement and on the life course. Differences in families' economic circumstances, however, may lead to major differences in this transition. Children from economically deprived circumstances may be deprived of an adolescence – that period of gradual transition from dependency to young adulthood – because they have to assume adult roles prematurely. We know that many students in Jamaica have to take on economic responsibility for their family, and boys are more likely to take on this responsibility than girls, mainly because there are more jobs in the informal sector for boys than girls. They may also be deprived of the normal protection usually given by family members. When students are required to play dual roles or take on roles that are usually associated with a different phase of the life cycle, it affects their participation in learning activities, in other activities of schooling, as well as the proper development of personality. Many young people in fact break the life cycle sequence completely – boys to work permanently, girls because of pregnancy. Many young people, especially boys, drop out of school not only because of economic hardships but because of the harsh treatment that they receive in school from teachers and students alike. Such interruptions have serious consequences for the life chances of the individual. Thus, schooling has differential benefits for individuals depending on economic and family circumstances as well as the conditions existing in their schools.

9

Our aims and our expectations suggest criteria for judging what takes place in schools. They also help us to formulate standards and to have vision of what schools should be like. What takes place in schools, however, does not always conform to these criteria. Practice very often falls short of these principles. The dual perspective of those who study schools stems from this tension between what should be and what is – between education and schooling. Schooling is what happens in schools and it may be educational; but very often it is not. This is so because schools are social settings created by individuals with different capacities and commitments, for ends which are sometimes elusive. Social settings create their own dynamics. Face-to-face interaction may further or subvert the educational goals of the school. Individuals may accept or be ambivalent about the goals. As social institutions, schools and the functioning of schools are subject to the vicissitudes of human and social behaviour. Parents, teachers, students, administrators come to this social setting with their own goals and expectations for school. Each is influenced in subtle ways by what society and the immediate community think about education and schooling. For some parents of young children, schools are not only places for their children to play and learn, but are also a safe place for their children to be while they are at work. Schools, therefore, have explicit goals; but they have latent goals as well, serving the purposes and the needs of the various groups associated with them.

Schools as institutions, therefore, cannot be studied as simple unitary entities. Willis (1978) has suggested that schools may be studied at three levels at least – the official or formal level with its official aims and purposes, and the pragmatic level where teachers and other staff reinterpret the official ideology of the school in order to cope with their own face-to-face problems of survival. At the third level are the students who bring with them their own personal experiences and expectations. These expectations vary according to the family and community from which the student comes and in turn interact with the requirements and purposes of the school. At this level, as we have seen, peer cultures develop that may work with or may thwart the goals of the first two levels. It is possible to add a fourth level – that of the parents and community members who also have expectations and who may work with or against the first two levels, depending on the issue at hand and the relationship established with the school.

Inside Schools

What is obvious about Jamaican schools is their diversity. There are different categories of schools created for different age levels and specializations. These schools were established at different historical periods. One type of school, the all-age school, has had a long history, going back to the establishment of a formal system of education in Jamaica. Others have been only recently established. The all-age school, then called the elementary school, was established soon after the abolition of slavery and was created only for the children of ex-slaves. Its purpose then was to provide rudimentary training and to prepare the children of ex-slaves to take their place as labourers in a rigidly stratified society (Turner, 1987). The first high school was established in 1887 for white children (King, 1987) who were meant to take a different place in society – as administrators and professionals.

The hand of history is evident today as these two schools are still extreme examples of the range of educational provisions. I have had the opportunity to visit an urban high school and an urban all-age school on the same day. On entering the grounds of the high school, one notices the clean surroundings, the trees and plants which beautify the setting, the walls which appear to be freshly painted, and the signs which direct the visitor to different sections of the campus. These signs suggest order. On entering the foyer in front of the general office, there are paintings of gentlemen in formal attire, who may have been former headmasters. One notices the clean, shiny, ceramic tiled floors and spaciousness. Inside the office, the secretaries are pleasant and helpful. At the all-age school, located in a commercial area of Kingston, handcarts vie with students and pedestrians for space on the sidewalks. There are about six or eight vendors who sit at the entrance outside the gate selling a variety of processed foods. At this entrance, students have to step over effluent in order to enter the premises. The campus appears cramped, except for the area in front which has no trees or signs. The two-storey buildings abut each other, with walls that look dirty and in need of paint. A student greets me in the office; an attendant points me to the principal's office. The classrooms are overcrowded, many students do not have chairs to sit on. This all-age school is less than a mile from the high school, but is distinctly different in almost every respect.

High schools which offer for the most part an academic curriculum are the preferred secondary schools for the vast majority of Jamaican parents,

11

and represent the best promise for upward social mobility. These schools were in most cases established under the auspices of the church and continue to have this association even though they are now run by the MOEC. In general, high schools have more resources and better qualified teachers than other types of schools. This is partly because of their high status relative to other schools and the support and the resources which these schools can obtain from past students. Historically the high schools received from the MOEC a higher per-student subvention than other types of schools. This historical advantage relative to other types of schools, as well as the circumstances under which they were established, help to explain the differences in the resources now evident in the high schools. Subventions, however, although superior, were never enough to meet the instructional needs of schools, which relied and still rely on the parents for any shortfall. Thus those schools whose parents had access to more resources (such as the high schools) could provide more resources for the school. The method of financing secondary schools was changed in the 1994–95 academic year. There is now a cost-sharing scheme which requires that parents pay a portion of the operational cost of running the school. However, high schools (now often referred to as the traditional high schools to distinguish them from the newly upgraded high schools) charge higher fees than other types of schools.[3]

High schools provide the most certain avenue to a university education, and are valued as educational institutions by employers and parents alike. The all-age school on the other hand is attended mainly by children of the lowest earning quintiles of the population. The all-age school serves as a primary and secondary school, as it offers instruction from Grades 1 to 9. As part of the ROSE programme, and the introduction of a new common curriculum at the Grades 7 to 9 levels, some all-age schools have been upgraded to become primary and junior high schools. The intent is to upgrade all-age schools to the status of primary and junior high schools (Grades 1 to 9), comprehensive high schools, or junior high schools. Although 40 percent of Jamaican students enrolled in Grades 7 to 9 are in all-age schools or those upgraded to primary and junior high schools, these schools are sometimes dismissed as an anachronism – an institution which should be abolished. Unlike the high school, many of whose graduates can go on to a university, students who attend the all-age school and the primary and junior high school have limited educational opportunities. Those who have not already dropped out are forced to leave school at an early age, with little hope of gaining entry to a

12

secondary school.[4] This stark reality no doubt affects the motivation of students and teachers alike to work hard and excel. Their uncertain future may affect students' attachment to their school. In 1991, one-third of a sample of all-age school students said they did not like their school (Evans, 1991).

These two types of schools have been described at some length in order to portray some of the differences among schools. The differences exist in their history, in the student body, the curriculum and exams sat, the resources available; and the co-curricular activities which are available. And as we have seen, there are also differences in the physical appearance and amenities, the look and feel of the surroundings – what Dreeben (1970) calls the ecology of the school. There are other types of schools at the secondary level. In addition to the all-age/primary and junior high schools, and the high schools, there are new secondary schools (now being phased out by the MOEC), comprehensive high schools, technical schools, and a few vocational and agricultural schools. At the primary level, there are public primary schools and private preparatory schools. There are small and large schools, rural schools, some serving very isolated farming communities. And there are large urban schools. Each of these categories defines the mission of the school. Each has its own ecology stemming from the kind of student body for which it caters, its location, the resources available, and the vision held for that school.

But while these schools differ by type, all these schools are similar in ways other than their common goal. They are influenced to varying degrees by social conditions and the values and attitudes of their immediate community. And they face shortages of resources which often affect teacher motivation, teaching methods, and student learning. The following descriptions of schools, written by research assistants who were part of a recent research study, capture the diversity of schools:

> This (high) school is located in rural St. Andrew. It is situated on a hill overlooking the valley. The school ground is clean with several trees planted. The air is fresh and clean and soothing. Teachers appear pleasant and encouraging. The classrooms are spacious and well ventilated with adequate furniture. Students appear friendly and well-behaved in their interactions with each other.
>
> This (all-age) school is located in the inner city and is surrounded by a variety of commercial activities. The school grounds are dusty. There are mural paintings in the yard. Some classrooms are

13

overcrowded, hot and dusty. There is a continuously high noise level. In the classroom observed, some students had to walk on desks to get to their seats. Some of the students (the boys) displayed antisocial behaviour.

This (primary) school is located in the inner city of Kingston seemingly hidden in the depth of a community polarized by violence and fear. The school is a two-storey building with a mural painting all over the ground floor. The teachers display much interest in the well-being of the students. The students themselves seem very quiet.

This (high) school is located in metropolitan _____. The school grounds are big and clean and shaded with trees. The classrooms are large, spacious and well ventilated, well lit, with adequate furniture. Each classroom is a separate entity divided by concrete walls. The students appear perceptive and outspoken. The teachers were helpful and displayed much interest in their students.

To understand what goes on in schools, we have to think of students, teachers, and administrators and their participation in the official purposes of school — i.e., teaching and learning. The administration, represented by the principal, creates a vision, sets the tone and climate and in a situation of severe financial constraints, finds resources for the school. It represents what Willis (1978) calls the official level of the school. Research conducted in industrialized countries tells us that the principal is a key figure in creating effective schools — by setting standards and expectations, and by motivating teachers. The principal, by his or her actions, words and deeds, by his or her commitment and enthusiasm, sense of caring for students and interest in creating good learning environments for all, can encourage teachers and parents to maintain standards and work towards goals. What the school's administration does at the official level will influence teachers and students and ultimately what occurs in the classroom. Our main interest in schools lies in classrooms and what occurs therein — the teachers, students, the curriculum and how they all interact to make up the stuff of education and schooling. To a large extent, what happens there affects students' attitude to school and to learning; it affects the kind of persons students become. What happens in classrooms also explains examination results, and whether students choose or are able to continue learning. Classrooms and schools are also places where society's tensions and conflicts are played out, and where identities are formed and contested. Education and schooling take place against a social and historical background. They are a very important formative influence in any society but especially in a postcolonial society. While we hold high hopes for education and our schools, students who attend these schools contend with the social and political issues which engage the wider society. To understand what happens in schools, we need to take all these issues into account. We also need to have a perspective on schools. The next chapter will discuss alternative theoretical perspectives in the study of schools.

2

Theoretical Perspectives
Approaches to Understanding and Studying Schools

A theoretical framework is simply a way of looking at or interpreting an issue, event, or situation. It provides a lens that offers a particular view of social situations, a view which is quite different from that seen when other theoretical frameworks are used. Our understanding of schools and how they work is usually couched in a theoretical framework, even though that theoretical framework is not always made explicit. In many cases, one makes certain assumptions without recognizing that there are alternative ways of looking at an issue related to education or schooling. Theoretical frameworks also provide a set of ideas or concepts for describing what exists and posits certain relationships among the elements in question. These ideas, concepts relationships and assumptions shape the way in which we analyse and interpret situations and are usually associated with a method of research.

There are competing theoretical frameworks or approaches to thinking about schools and understanding what goes on in them. Some focus on the human agent or actor acting in particular social situations, and attempt to understand how particular actions and interactions define social reality from the actor's point of view. These approaches share certain assumptions about social reality. They assume that social relations between persons are constantly being *constituted* or *structured*. Each person, regardless of his or her place in the social system, contributes to the relations or the structuring of those relations through his or her cooperation, sentiments, acquiescence, definition of the situation, resistance to the status quo and so on. For example, a conversation between two persons is determined not only by their status vis-à-vis each other (teacher/student, employer/employee) but by the attitudes and sentiments they have toward each other, their past experiences and conversations, and the history of the relations between the social or ethnic groups to which each belongs. At the same time, each person is formed by those social relations and social interactions. Over time through such interactions and social relations occurring in institutions such as the family or the school, one's identity, attitudes and sentiments are formed. Culture, therefore – ways of behaving and interacting, views about the situation and the wider society – is always being produced or created. Thus, it becomes important to know the meaning perspectives of actors in particular settings – their goals, expectations, needs, definitions and assumptions, the meaning of events and interactions to ordinary people in particular situations, and the subjective aspects of people's behaviour (Erickson, 1986; Bogdan and Biklen, 1998).

Cultural production is one of the theoretical approaches in this tradition. Educators and researchers who adopt this approach have tended to focus on students and their experiences in schools, the basis and goals of their friendship groups or associations. They also examine the extent to which these groups function in harmony with or opposition to the values of the school and the rules and regulations laid down by teachers and administrators. Researchers who adopt this perspective on schools and schooling have found that students who come from different classes and ethnic groups may bring to the school an ideology, their own cultural forms, practices and community values. These ideas, expectations and behaviours may bring these students in conflict with some aspects of the school as well as with other students. They may introduce tensions into the relationship between teachers and administrators, and themselves. Willis (1978) in his study of working class youth in a British secondary school found that "the most basic, obvious and explicit dimension of counter-school culture is entrenched general and personalized opposition to authority" (p. 11) – an inversion of the usual values of diligence and respect held up by authority.

Educators and researchers with a cultural production perspective are interested in understanding this form of students' behaviour that arises in response to aspects of the school's functioning and organization, the

17

reasons for this response, and the extent to which this response is shaped by the students' home and community culture. They are also interested in the effects such behaviour may have on the students, on their developing identity, and on student/teacher relationships. The perspective of cultural production has the potential for revealing the range of identities that students develop while they are in school, and the masculinities and femininities that are constructed as a result of the school experience. The construction of such identities can be seen in the recent work of Connell, 1996; Mac an Ghaill, 1994; Gilborn, 1998; and Sewell, 1999.

Another perspective in this tradition is that of cultural studies. This approach to interpreting society and social events also focuses on students' behaviour within the context of the school, but goes beyond the concerns of cultural production. Educators or researchers whose work is influenced and informed by this perspective have a commitment to examining cultural practices from the point of view of power relations, the process of struggle for those who do not have power or who are marginalized within a system. They are also concerned about the ways in which such persons can be given voice and empowerment. Cultural studies, as a way of interpreting social reality, grew out of the efforts of some individuals in England who were outside the English white Anglo-Saxon mainstream and who sought to find a place in a society that was itself changing. It also grew out of their critique of the power relations of that society, particularly with respect to class and race. "Cultural studies insists on the necessity to address the central, urgent, and disturbing questions of a society" (Hall, 1996: 337). The various cultures in a postcolonial society have a history of relationships with each other — usually one of dominance, subordination and control. The struggle for equality, recognition and transformation of attitudes is therefore an important aspect of the cultural studies project (Stratton and Ang, 1996).

Because of the link between the concerns of cultural studies and the legacy of colonialism or dominant/subordinate relations, a postcolonial perspective is sometimes combined with a cultural studies perspective by some third world educators. Postcolonial theory, which has had a strong influence on literary and cultural studies, is an approach to understanding and interpreting societies which have passed through the colonial experience and the many contradictions and complexities that present themselves as a result of this experience. It recognizes that colonialism left enduring marks on those societies that experienced it — societies stratified by race, class and colour where certain attitudes formed during the colonial period still linger. In the area of education, this perspective can be very useful in examining a range of issues, such as aspects of the curriculum and textbooks, differential access to education for different social and racial groups, the language that is used in schools and the value placed on the indigenous languages of students (Hickling-Hudson, 1998; Tikly, 1998). It also examines attitudes such as the valuing of what is European, and the stigmatization of some social and racial groups which can have a negative influence on students' self-esteem, self-confidence, identity, and overall development. The social and historical legacy of Jamaican schools makes a postcolonial perspective very relevant to the study of Jamaican schools and what happens in them. When cultural studies is combined with a postcolonial perspective, it recognizes the inequalities that now exist as a result of the colonial experience, the legacies of having subordinate and dominant groups based on race, the attributions of superiority and inferiority on the basis of that dominance and subordination, the continued existence of such attitudes, and the pervasiveness of Eurocentric values. It examines all aspects of education and schooling that may manifest these influences including the curriculum, the teacher/pupil relationship, the nature of discourse between teachers and students and among students, school practices, and the content of rules and regulations. Because it has foregrounded the working class and issues related to race, cultural studies when applied to education in a postcolonial context, turns the gaze on the experiences of those who are marginalized – students from poor or working-class homes – and the ways in which colour, class and gender influence these experiences.

Education in Jamaica is a rich site for cultural studies analysis with a postcolonial perspective. Originally a dual system of education was established for whites and blacks and it is only within the last twenty to thirty years that this dual system has been dismantled. Although the curriculum has now been made Caribbean, there are still debates in the society about the value of some of the cultural forms of the Jamaican folk and their place in the curriculum. Some persons value what is British or white or foreign over what is Jamaican or African. The Jamaican Creole language is still viewed in pathological terms, and regarded as "bad English" which must be avoided if one wants to be seen as educated. Moreover, there continue to be attitudes toward blackness and to local cultural forms that range from ambivalence to negativism. As Meeks (1996) has stated, "the culture of slavery still casts its shadow over the entire Caribbean" (p. 3). In such a society, much of what takes place in education and schooling is contested. Teachers and students bring to school attitudes abroad in the society; contradictions and conflicts get played out in face-to-face inter-action and in decision making about standards and behaviour in schools. Within such an environment, it becomes very difficult for students – par-ticularly adolescents – to establish an identity and a firm sense of self.

Cultural production and cultural studies can be contrasted with other approaches to the study of society or social reality, which begin not with the individuals' perspectives and experiences but with an articulation of how society functions. Such an articulation represents a model of what society should be and this model is like a system. Of these macro-sociological approaches, the one that has been most influential is that of structuralism, sometimes referred to as structural-functionalism. Structural functionalists assume that social structure or the social system is analysable in components such as social· values, norms, and roles that individuals play in various situations. The sociologist or educator with this perspective is particularly interested in the ways in which each social sub-system carries out its functions and the contribution of that subsystem to the entire society. Because structural functionalists assume that each part of the social system should work toward equilibrium and maintain order, they are interested in making prescriptions about preferred or desirable procedures, which promise to achieve outcomes necessary for the system as a whole. It is usual for structural functionalists to analyse educational issues by examining the inputs and the outputs to the system. These inputs include social categories such as ethnic group, race, or social class, and academic ability as measured by intelligence tests. Because these are considered the main social "inputs" to education, educational outcomes are often explained in terms of these social categories.

Structural functionalism assumes that there is a consensus on what the functions of society or institutions are. It is also assumed that the structures or the institutions act in benign or unbiased ways to perform its functions and that these structures have similar effects on individuals (Karabel and Halsey, 1977). In education, it assumes that there is a consensus on the benefits and the value of education and schooling, as well as on what is to be taught. The state, i.e. the MOEC, determines what is valuable, and what knowledge should be learned; the citizens are assumed to have the same opinion. Maintaining the social order is of supreme importance and this framework assigns to the school the role of moulding the individual to fit into the social order. The structural-functional framework regards schools as neutral, even benign, institutions of a neutral state; such institutions are charged with maintaining and passing on society's values. This liberal view of schooling assumes that schools distribute their rewards according to individual merit. Success in school depends on the ability and motivation of the student. Those who are less able or motivated are less likely to succeed. And those who do not succeed are less able or motivated.

The belief in education as a means of upward mobility for all, or at least for those individuals with merit, rests on these assumptions. These assumptions about schools inform much policy and public debate about schools. It also informs much research in education, including sociological and psychological studies on the relationship between students' characteristics and certain outcomes of schools. This view of schooling has been most influential in the sociology of education and is the one most often used to explain the outcomes and the workings of schools. Examples of the use of structural functionalism to analyse education and schooling in Jamaica may be found in the reader *Sociology of Education* by Figueroa and Persaud (1976). In their introduction to this book, Persaud and Figueroa discuss four sociological "models" of society. Nevertheless, most of the articles in that reader reflect the assumptions of structural functionalism and an input/output or production function approach to formulating educational issues and research questions. A large proportion of the papers in the reader are concerned with inputs such as social class, ethnicity and race, sex roles, family size, the type of family headship, the educational environment of the home, and achievement values (p. 22). The structural functionalist perspective has been heavily criticized because it assumes that there is consensus in society when in fact there is much conflict; it pays little attention to the content and process of education; and it ignores motivations and individual interests and perspectives. Missing also is any critique of the school as an institution, though individual teachers may be criticized.

Another macro-sociological approach to studying schools is the social reproduction theory based on the conflict model of schooling. Conflict models assert that there are inherent conflicts among different groups in a society – especially between those who are powerful and with economic resources and those who are not. The social reproduction theory asserts that schools are instrumental in allocating or sorting students to take different places in the economic system. This sorting is often done not according to individual merit, but according to the social class or race of the individual (e.g., Apple, 1972, 1996; Bowles and Gintis, 1976;

Karabel and Halsey, 1977). This critique of schools came especially from Marxists who saw schools as engaging in social reproduction on the basis of class. These theorists underscore the very political role which schools play in any society, since schools directly affect the life chances of individuals and serve to allocate persons to various roles and positions in society.

Conflict models have not been extensively used to analyse education in Jamaica. One example of this, however, is Goulbourne's historical study of the development of teachers' associations in Jamaica. His description of the circumstances surrounding the establishment of the Jamaica Union of Teachers (JUT) in 1894 focuses on the conflict which existed between the elementary teachers and a white colonial establishment. The conflict found expression in low levels of support for education, inadequate provisions and resources, and restricted access to decision making on the part of the teachers. These were some of the circumstances which led to the formation of the JUT. During the 1960s and 1970s, these conflicts between teachers and the state became more "political", focusing on issues of autonomy, representation on decision-making bodies and salaries. The conflict model has also been used by Miller (1991) to explain the gender differences in academic achievement at the school level, as well as the relative and recent advancement of women in the workplace. Miller contends that there is a basic and ongoing struggle between certain racial and social groups in society. More specifically, small groups of males at the higher levels of society wish to keep lower class men and boys in a menial position. To do this, they move women into positions of power or responsibility in order to keep these men "marginalized".

Goulbournes's study focuses on teachers' associations, while Miller's thesis is applied mainly to gender differences in access and achievement. If one were to apply a conflict model to educational practice, one would examine the regularities of schooling – all activities performed on a regular basis in the service of education, such as planning, teaching, testing, streaming, and so on. Since practices do not exist without procedures, rules, assumptions, choices, values, and interests, one would study all these aspects of schooling to determine whether they reveal existing systematic differences with respect to class, race, gender or any other characteristic which is accorded some value. For example, we know that differences exist among different types of schools, that different levels of resources are made available to some schools and that there are differences in the curriculum which each type of school offers. Based on this information, one could argue that the state and its representatives base these decisions on the numbers and categories of workers needed by employers, and would legitimize certificates based on employers' preferences. One could argue, if one accepted the reproduction theory, that the number of these schools reflects what is expected of children in each social stratum.

A major methodological problem with conflict theories is that they argue *ex post facto*. One has to speculate on the decision-making processes and the assumptions of policy makers which led to the existing unequal outcomes. Rarely are scholars and researchers privy to empirical data about these decisions and assumptions, except in the case of historical studies such as that done by Goulbourne. Furthermore, conflict theories ignore or de-emphasize the importance of individual human agency. For example, Miller's thesis accords very little importance to the will, motivation, drive, and decision-making capability of women and girls who may individually want to change and improve their circumstances. In addition, they do not allow for differences within a social group, such as teachers, students or powerful men. And they have a simplistic view of schools as instruments of the state or society. While the conflict argument may be plausible, the inequality may also be a consequence of the indifference on the part of policy makers to the condition of the poorer classes of society or to men or women, rather than planned differentiation based on social class, race or gender. It could also be a result of a lack of understanding of the ways in which one can bring about educational change. Or the differences may be due to realities that are socially constructed by the individuals themselves as the cultural production theorists would argue. Nevertheless, because of the stratified nature of the education system and of the Jamaican society, and the history of separateness and discrimination, the educational system is a promising site for analysis from the perspective of conflict theories.

Although many conflict theorists have not supported their theories with empirical research, some researchers have carried out research framed by this perspective and attempted to show how schools have these effects. An example is the research on organizational practices such as streaming or tracking (e.g. Oakes, 1985; Page, 1989) which shows how curriculum varies according to the student's social class. But the overly deterministic view of schooling and the absence of human agency or the individual perspective in this theoretical framework has led others who are critical of how schools function to look for other explanations for what happens in schools.

Another conflict theory and an alternative approach to understanding schools and how they work is closely related to social reproduction theory and is called cultural reproduction theory. It recognizes the role that schools play in the reproduction of the cultural bases of privilege. This view of schooling states that society and schools value the knowledge, cultural styles, and behaviours of a select group. Schools regard the culture and knowledge of this group as more prestigious, and select it for the formal curriculum. The knowledge and cultural forms associated with this privileged group or social class becomes "cultural capital", similar to economic capital in the benefits which it confers (Bourdieu, 1977; Bourdieu and Passeron, 1977). These theorists see schools as sites of cultural reproduction. Power relations and differences in cultural values and knowledge are reproduced within the school at the level of practice and in face-to-face interaction. Within discursive practices – i.e., talk among students and between students and teachers, some students – the "non-élite" develop a "sense of their social limits". As these limits are learned or internalized, these students learn to self-censor and to self-silence in the presence of those with more cultural stature.

Those who adopt a cultural reproduction approach to analysing schools focus on the curriculum and the kind of knowledge and symbolic capital which is excluded and that which is seen as legitimate. They also examine rituals, ceremonies, language, dress, and other cultural expressions which may be excluded or allowed within the school. In Jamaica, there have been practices which could be interpreted from a cultural reproduction perspective. For example, there have been many instances where the children of Rastafarians have been excluded from school on the basis of their hairstyle or headgear, and having a haircut has been made the condition for entry to the school. And there are many individuals and groups in the Jamaican society who have for a long time criticized the exclusion of the thoughts of Marcus Garvey from the official curriculum of the primary and secondary schools. These and other practices can be interpreted from a cultural reproduction perspective. The social reproduction and cultural reproduction theories have been termed conflict theories, as their basic assumption is that the social groups which make up society have different interests and seek to pursue those interests. Those who have more power or resources will strive to maintain or increase their position at the expense of others. This places social groups in conflict with each other.

Theoretical Perspectives and Related Approaches to Research

Educational researchers have been influenced by one or more of the theoretical perspectives described above and each perspective has been associated with particular research methods. The structural functional perspective has been associated with research methods borrowed from the natural sciences. These methods were used by researchers in the natural sciences who sought to discover law-like relations among elements, and to make generalizations on the basis of these relations.[1] Educational research in this tradition assumes that the purpose of educational research is, as in the natural sciences, to discover knowledge of law-like regularities which can then be applied to educational practice. However, although most researchers with this perspective have used this method of research, it is possible to be influenced by this perspective and use a qualitative research method. For example, Piaget's ideas on cognitive development were influenced by structuralism (Piaget, 1968), yet he used qualitative observation to obtain data that informed his theory of cognitive development.

The conflict theories – social reproduction and cultural reproduction – have not been associated with any one research method. Researchers who subscribe to this view of schooling have chosen research methods typical of the positivist paradigm as well as ethnographic and other qualitative approaches. So for example, Keith (1976) in her study of socialization of students of different social and ethnic groups in the Jamaican primary school used correlational indices to determine the relationship between these social inputs, student participation, and educational outcomes. On the other hand, Anyon (1981) and Jones (1989) with similar objectives used participant observation and interviewing methods to determine that students participate differentially in the educational process and hence achieve different educational outcomes.

The cultural production and cultural studies perspectives have been associated with qualitative approaches to studying schools and schooling. The term qualitative refers to a variety of methods that focus on subjective meanings, experiences, and the influence of the context and the culture. These methods require long-term stay in the field, since researchers want to gain an in-depth understanding of social interactions over time. Various terms are used to refer to these methods such as ethnography, case study, and anthropological research. The main methods of data collection are

25

participant observation which allows the researcher to understand the culture and ways of life of those studied. An example of this type of research is found in Seaga's (1955) study of parent/teacher relationships in a Jamaican village. He used these methods to reveal some of the tensions between teachers and parents, the expectations and misunderstandings which parents held, and some of the teaching practices which existed in rural Jamaica in the 1950s.

Ethnographers regard the school and the classroom as environments where reality is socially constructed by those who interact therein. As such, they investigate school and classroom phenomena up close, combining "close analysis of fine details of behavior and meaning in everyday social interaction with analysis of the wider social context" (Erickson, 1986: 120). They assume that teachers and students co-construct knowledge, understandings, and ways of interacting. They investigate the ways in which the broader social, cultural, and historical context of the society affects what goes on in school. Ethnographic research rests firmly in the interpretive tradition of social inquiry that "seeks to replace scientific notions of explanation, prediction and control, with the interpretive notions of understanding, meaning and action" (Carr and Kemmis, 1986: 83).

The empirical evidence from ethnographic research has made it evident that what happens in schools is much more complex than what is implied by structural functionalism, and social or cultural reproduction theory. Power and control in schools and the relationship between teacher and student are not necessarily as simple or uni-directional as once thought. Students — at least some of them — resist such practices. The efforts of students — especially secondary students — to develop a sense of personal autonomy and a personal, racial, class or gender identity have to be accommodated in any explanation of schools and schooling. A cultural production approach to understanding schools accords importance to the students' perspective and the often conflicting relationship which exists between these students, their social, ethnic or racial groups, and the school. It assumes that the conflicts get played out in practice and in social interactions. These conflicts exist in part because of the differences that often exist between the home and community of some students and those of the teachers. In a sense, these differences may be explained by cultural reproduction theory. However, those with a cultural reproduction perspective do take a deterministic view, assuming that all teachers and all students from a particular class or cultural group will be in conflict.

The choice of theoretical perspective and an associated research method has been important in my own development as an educator and researcher. Combining research interests with a research method occurred naturally. As a doctoral student, I was fortunate to take a qualitative research methods course, which turned out to be much more relevant to what I wanted to do than the three quantitative research methods that were a mandatory part of the doctoral programme. Prior to my entry to the programme, I had developed an interest in teaching and learning as a teacher of adults, and this interest was compatible with a qualitative approach to research. Professional interest thus combined naturally with research interest. This interest in quality teaching has continued and now informs my work as a teacher educator. It also influences my choice of research topics. These roles keep me in constant touch with schools, teachers, and students and has allowed me to observe teaching in Jamaica in a variety of contexts.

Developing a theoretical perspective linked to research interests and method evolved over a period of time. Like most graduate students in the 1970s, my training in the field of education was heavily influenced by structural functionalism, the dominant perspective in the sociology and psychology of education at the time. I accepted all that I read in this tradition. I accepted the liberal views regarding the emancipatory and equalizing effects of education and schooling, even though I saw contradictory evidence all around me. I realized later that those assumptions were not the bases on which the educational system in Jamaica was established and that the legacy of that beginning has not been completely eradicated. My first research in schools in Jamaica was an ethnographic study of all-age schools. It was a descriptive study of what goes on in those schools — how teachers teach, how students learn and do not learn, the resources available and the perspectives of parents, teachers, and students. It opened my eyes to what life in disadvantaged schools is like for students and teachers alike. It showed me the ways in which students from the poor and working classes are badly served by education and the limits that are placed on their future as a result. The study, however, was not informed by a theoretical perspective. Today, I frequently visit schools as teacher educator or researcher and I have become familiar with life in schools. I enter schools with more than one perspective — as researcher, teacher and teacher educator. Based on my knowledge of schools, I have come to believe that the cultural production perspective has promise for illuminating the students' culture and the ways in which their experiences in school, home, and community influence their learning and consequently their life chances.

Yet, I have had other experiences in schools that show the potential value not only of examining the formation of identity but also of examining these issues together with the issues of power and empowerment and the effects of race, class, and gender. I recall my observation of a little girl in a Grade 3 class which I was observing in the 1980s. She was small and seemed timid – almost fearful. She never said a word in class. Her seat was near the back and in the corner where I sat to observe. I kept noticing her and kept thinking that she needed some encouragement, hoping that the teacher (with a class of fifty students) would notice her and show some encouragement. One day, the students were asked to draw a picture of themselves and to describe themselves in the drawing. This little girl drew a picture of herself the size of a medium-sized safety pin; it was drawn to the bottom of the page. The drawing she made of herself had no hands and showed very little detail on the face. The drawing was simply there on the otherwise blank page. I asked her to tell me about the little girl, but she said nothing. I still have the image in my mind of this frightened little girl who rarely spoke and who thought she was only as significant as a little pin at the bottom of a blank page. I have thought about her very often since then. I have come to realize through a child's drawing of herself that there is a strong connection among parental treatment, home experiences, being wanted and cared for, identity, self-concept, social relationships with peers, being accepted, self-acceptance, participation in learning activities, and ultimately learning and academic achievement. In many cases, these issues are related to race, class, and gender. The perspective of cultural studies allows one to look deeper beneath the surface of students' culture and behaviour, interrogating relationships of the individual's sense of self, power, voice, and representation. As such, I believe it offers promise for gaining more knowledge about schools' and students' experiences. It also allows a more critical look at school practices, describing what exists as well as comparing it with a vision of the possible.

At the same time, as one who grew up in colonial Jamaica, socialized with the old and the new values, and in particular, as one who frequently observes postcolonial legacies and contradictions in schools and classrooms, I recognize the value of having a postcolonial lens to examine what transpires in education. A postcolonial perspective highlights the issues foregrounded by cultural studies, but examines them within the legacy of colonialism. It can be used to examine school practices with these issues in mind and, in so doing, determine who has voice, who exercises power, and how authority is exercised. Above all, it can turn the gaze on those who have been disadvantaged by the experience of colonialism and the quality of their interpersonal encounters.

Adopting a cultural production or a cultural studies perspective on schools points to a new relation between social theory, research and practice (Wexler, 1987). When we adopt these perspectives, we move from the liberal faith in rationality, law-like relations, predictability, and control (promised by structural-functionalism) to a "centring" of the individual, and of students' subjectivity. Adopting these perspectives also raises new challenges for the educator. How can education and schooling benefit from the knowledge of how individuals or different groups respond to educational practices? What do we do with the knowledge that teachers create inequality on the basis of the students' personal characteristics and place of residence, for example? What do we do about the black girl who is too afraid to speak and who from a drawing sees herself as insignificant? We shall examine some of these challenges in the research that will be examined in this volume and at the end, discuss the challenge that these issues pose for schools, research, and theory.

Inside Classrooms
Teachers, Students and Authority

We can think of the class as a temporary mini-society which exists for a period of a year. Teachers and students have to establish a relationship with one another, and in other ways create a social setting. The teacher is a key figure in initiating and creating this setting. The sentiments which teachers and students have toward one another are critical to this relationship and become the basis for successful efforts at teaching and learning. The classroom is also the setting for students to experience the curriculum. What happens in classrooms is also shaped by the cultural context – the society's expectations and the standards it applies to schools, teaching, and the outcomes of schooling.

Teachers

Like schools, teachers are a diverse lot. They vary in their level of qualification, the subjects they teach, and the level at which they teach. They also differ in their commitment to teaching and the reasons why they chose teaching in the first place. Some decided to enter teaching because of the nature of teaching itself and the possibility which the profession offers of providing service and influencing young minds. The idea of giving service and of working with children was a major factor in the decision of many to become a teacher. Many were influenced by a former teacher or by a relative who was a teacher, and many entered the profession by default – because they believed no other option was available (Brown, 1992; Evans, 1993). This is not very different from the reasons given by teachers elsewhere (Lortie, 1975: 27; Goodlad, 1984: 171; Johnson, 1990: 33). Many teachers also decided to enter the profession or at least to go to a teachers' college because of the limited opportunities available at the tertiary level.[1] Teachers have varying commitments to teaching and those who enter teaching because of limited opportunities available in the society, or who regard college as a stepping stone, may not remain in the profession for a very long period of time.

When teachers are mentioned in the public discourse on education, their shortcomings are often highlighted. Criticism of teachers stems from our high expectations for schools as well as from the memory of our own teachers. Many of us have an idealized image of our former teachers; the behaviour, conduct, and performance of contemporary teachers fall short of what we can recall of our own teachers. The fact that teaching appears easy, and does not appear to require any special knowledge, partly explains such criticism. "Everyone feels a certain legitimacy and authority in commenting on education, derived from their many years in school . . ." (Lightfoot, 1983: 243). Such criticism may also reflect the lowered public esteem in which teachers are held. Anecdotal accounts suggest that in the past in Jamaica, people rarely criticized teachers. If one had reservations about the teacher's judgment or behaviour, such thoughts were kept private. The present public criticism reflects changes in the general esteem in which teachers are held and such changes have profound effects upon the way teachers experience their jobs. This reduced public esteem and a general loss of professional self-respect can have a devastating effect on the teacher's morale and level of satisfaction (Ball and Goodson, 1985: 2).

Despite this propensity on the part of the public to evaluate teachers and teaching, it is difficult to agree on the criteria on which such evaluations should be made. This is because there is no "unequivocal definition of teaching that holds true for all time and all places" (Jackson, 1986: 95), and because teaching requires a combination of skill and social and interpersonal competence. Teaching is also influenced to a great degree by the teachers' values and personality. This combination of skills, values, and interpersonal competence makes it hard to disentangle teacher character from teacher competence. Although many have tried to reduce teaching to a set of skills or routines, such efforts can only account for a fraction of what is important in explaining a teacher's effectiveness. This characteristic of teaching in part explains the "endemic uncertainties" (Lortie, 1975)

31

which teachers face in their work. This uncertainty about the work, the absence of direct and immediate evidence about outcomes, and a lack of other rewards may lead to teacher unease if not dissatisfaction. The intense and continuous involvement of the self in this work may lead to "teacher burnout".

In the literature on education, teachers are often represented as statistics, such as the number of teachers in the various types of school, the percentage who are professionally qualified or untrained, or the number who have a university degree and so on. In much of the research in education, teachers are often portrayed as role incumbents, performing certain functions which contribute to the outcomes of schooling. In the more conventional research on teaching in Jamaica, attributes of the teacher such as age, sex, qualification, and years of experience, or pedagogical and psychological variables such as teaching style and locus of control are examined to see their relationship with some outcomes of interest (for reviews of such research, see Hamilton, 1991; Evans, 1994; Miller, 1997). On the other hand, the way teachers experience teaching – their satisfaction, morale, and the rewards which they gain from teaching – relate to the self and the inner life. When teachers talk about their work and their career, it is these psychic rewards which they mention. And given the nature of teaching, this is not surprising. Many researchers have found that teachers get their rewards from exchanges with students and their influence on a young life. They take satisfaction in giving service (Lortie, 1975; Ball and Goodson, 1985; Feiman-Nemser and Floden, 1986). Teaching, of course, has other rewards which have been categorized as extrinsic – for example, status, prestige, money, and power – and intrinsic or psychic, which relate to such matters as working hours and relations with colleagues. Traditionally teachers have not been expected to seek extrinsic rewards such as money, power, and status. However, such expectations change with time and differ by geography and social context. Individual teachers also vary in the importance they attach to such matters. In any event, teachers have rarely been paid high salaries or been seen as powerful. Teachers themselves do not see themselves as powerful (Feiman-Nemser and Floden, 1986) although they can have such a profound effect on the minds of the young. Teachers' satisfaction has traditionally come from the learning or achievement of their students – especially the outstanding achiever. Ancillary rewards such as conditions of work or relations with colleagues may also have an effect on a teacher's satisfaction. These aspects of the teacher's professional life are also related to the prospects for a long-term career in teaching.

Another characteristic that may influence a teacher's satisfaction is the lack of opportunities for advancement or for taking on new responsibilities on the job. Teaching is an "unstaged career" with a fairly flat organizational structure. This means that vertical advancement is virtually non-existent. The staff positions in most schools are not very differentiated; while there may be some senior teachers, coordinators or heads of departments, and more recently master teachers, they constitute a small portion of the staff. Promotion to principal or vice-principal is open to only a few. Consequently, opportunities for vertical advancement, while a teacher, are limited. When experienced teachers want new responsibilities or challenges, or develop new interests, they face a dilemma, for they form deep attachments to their students. They therefore have to abandon these interests or abandon the classroom. There is evidence, however, that some teachers do not regard career continuity or the traditional advancement "up the career ladder" as important characteristics of their work. Many who choose to enter teaching and to remain in teaching do so because of the service they can provide, the intrinsic rewards they gain (Lortie, 1975; Lightfoot, 1983; Feiman-Nemser and Floden, 1986; Brown, 1992). These teachers will continue in teaching as long as they continue to obtain the rewards which they expected.

The "flatness" of the occupational structure has led many to highlight the sameness of the teacher's work. The twenty-year veteran has the same job description as the neophyte, it is argued. However, there is much evidence that teachers over time experience their work differently. They develop different perspectives on teaching, learning, students, and even the curriculum. The teacher goes through different stages, each of which is characterized by a different way of thinking, different concerns, and different needs. The teacher's thinking changes over time. Their understanding of the subject matter deepens and their practical knowledge about classrooms and students' learning grows. Experience, reflection on one's experience, learning from other colleagues, and further education can all help the teacher to refine knowledge about the various aspects of the work. Such development, however, is not automatic. The teacher, like the student, thrives in a nurturing environment: characteristics of the workplace, and opportunities for reflection and collaboration are vital for this teacher growth.

What are the rewards which teaching offers teachers today? What are the occupational rewards which Jamaican teachers expect? Can they obtain these rewards, given the social and economic changes which have occurred in Jamaica in recent years? How do the facts of teaching life – lack of opportunities for vertical advancement, low salaries – affect male and female teachers? Do they influence a teacher's satisfaction? Are they considerations in their decision to remain in the profession? Coke (1991) examined the psychic rewards of teaching in the 1980s and the ways in which some Jamaican teachers at the time thought about aspects of their work. In her study of six teachers, Coke learned about some of the rewards of teaching and the ways in which certain characteristics of the profession affect the way teachers think about their work. She also learned about the ways in which society's valuation of the profession affects teachers' feelings of satisfaction about their work. In her study, she interviewed six former high school teachers who left the profession during the 1980s, a period when the profession and the society itself underwent major social and economic changes. The retrospective look at their decision to leave provided all six teachers with the opportunity to reflect on their teaching career from a distance. This distance provided these teachers with a perspective which teachers rarely have and which now allows us to see over time, the changes in their experience and their thinking about themselves, their priorities, and the profession. We get a glimpse of their career needs, their personal goals and aspirations, the ways in which their personal and professional lives intersected, and the priorities which developed over time.

The six interviewees – four women and two men – were in their thirties and forties at the time of the interviews; with years of experience ranging from six to twenty years. The author, herself a former teacher, described the process of decision making and the stages which the teachers underwent before finally deciding to leave. The process of decision making is described as long, deliberate, and agonizing, and is depicted in five stages – from entry to the profession to the final decision to leave. At stage one – entry to teaching, the teachers varied in their commitment to the profession. Five had had no professional qualification, two had made no conscious choice about a career; another had entered teaching on the suggestion of a church member. For most of these teachers therefore, teaching was something that they were trying out. Since almost all of them did not have any professional teacher training, they were not committed to the profession. At stage two – initiation into the classroom, there is enthusiasm about the work of teaching and a realization that what they do is meaningful and exciting. A commitment to teaching begins to develop.

At stage three – a time when these teachers were in their late twenties or early thirties, they began to feel "mild feelings of unease", "vague misgiving" or a "sense of dissatisfaction". This is a time in the life cycle when "life becomes more serious . . . it becomes more important to plan a life structure" (Sikes, 1985: 44). Some of the teachers began to look to the future and to consider the possibilities for advancement or further challenge within the profession. Involvement in the deeper concerns of her adolescent students made one of these teachers begin to question the relevance and importance of the subject matter which she was teaching. Parallel developments in their personal lives and especially the question of financial adequacy created further questions about the desirability of staying in the profession.

At stage four, social attitudes toward teachers, their own self-esteem and sense of self as professionals became important considerations in their decision to leave the profession. This was a time during the 1970s and 1980s, when there was a deterioration not only in the physical conditions in schools but in society's attitudes toward teachers and teaching. More and more of their friends and relatives began to feel that those with ambition sought their fulfilment elsewhere. As the question "Are you still teaching?" was asked more and more frequently, their vague unease became more profound. Changes in the behaviour and attitudes of students and fellow teachers alike, "economic deprivation", erosion in their self-esteem, an exodus of their own friends from the profession, combined with a loss of societal regard, made the teachers think more seriously and more often of an alternative career. We see that for the two men in this study, their financial situation was a deciding factor, while for the women, three of whom were married, it was just one consideration. Nevertheless, at this stage, they were for the most part still grounded in teaching and still involved with the cycle of school activities – teaching, interacting with students, examinations, marking scripts. They had decided to leave, but the manner and timing of their departure were still open questions. Coke presents the final stage as one of "conflict, guilt and departure". Such emotional reactions are often seen when one leaves the human service occupations (Sikes,1985), and it is especially marked among teachers who have to interact with young people.

The extracts below from Coke's study offer glimpses of teachers progression along these stages:

Stage 2 – Early commitment and enthusiasm

In all cases the initiation into the profession had produced enthusiasm. For Sharie,[2] this enthusiasm was reflected in her quickened speech and gestures as we relived her early feelings:

> I wanted to teach! I wanted to teach Spanish!
> I was highly motivated; I had taught what my tutors had described as a spectacular Spanish lesson during teaching practice. I went in thinking all my lessons would be like that one . . .

Arlene and Colin both entered teaching without having made conscious choices about a career and also without teacher training. Nonetheless, on reflection, both admitted that within a short time, they had been struck by a sense that what they had become involved in was meaningful and exciting:

> One of the things that really grabbed me was getting a remedial student and bringing him to a level where he was better than those not classified as such: Another thing was being met in the street by a student who recognized you and showed appreciation . . . (Colin)

Arlene recalled the feeling of excitement at playing the role her own favourite teacher had played for her:

> I was given the same Literature book to teach as she had taught me. I remembered the excitement she had displayed about Shakespeare and how she had caught my interest. I realized I had an opportunity to do the same thing for those boys and it was a challenge . . .

The secondary teacher's affiliation with and enthusiasm for his or her specialist subject was also a consideration. Respondents confirmed the assertion of Sikes (1985) that at the stage of entry to the profession,

> . . . the subject is usually personally very important. Most teachers have to a greater or lesser degree of intensity, a special fondness for and get a great deal of enjoyment from their subject.

It was borne out in my discussions that the early enthusiasm had to do with the desire to share with students a subject which a teacher had found exciting or which was considered critical to the development of the young mind. In addition, they derived a level of confidence from their own knowledge of the subject:

> *I felt that my knowledge of English was good enough and that my enthusiasm about opening their eyes to the beauty of literary experience would do the rest . . .* (Arlene)

Some of these initial positive reactions to the teaching role were reinforced by other factors in the wider society. Al recalled that this was at a time when society's attitude to the teacher was much better:

> *Even though the traditional reverence had been eroded somewhat the teacher was still regarded as an important asset.*

Stage 3 – Questioning and early misgivings

The process by which these initial feelings of enthusiasm and commitment are displaced by dissatisfaction began at different stages and ages. Nonetheless, all respondents shared the view that it was a long and sometimes indistinct process characterized by vacillation, guilt, and the impact of other factors, as well as certain types of critical incidents. In the process, a variety of influential factors operated at various times for each person. Teachers do not seem to leave the profession during the period of early misgivings. It appears rather, that there is first of all a relatively mild feeling of unease . . . a sense that perhaps something is not quite in place:

> *It's as if you begin to lose the conviction that this is really what you want and believe in; even though at first you are not quite sure why you feel this way . . .* (Arlene)

These early stirrings appear to have been associated with certain events including personal "life-stage" transition, shifts in personal philosophy, and changing domestic conditions. This is seen in the responses of some of the respondents. Arlene spoke of vague misgivings. Others pinpointed specific causes which could nevertheless be symptomatic of a "passage". For Al, it was the broadening of his own intellectual horizons beyond what he believed would be properly challenged in teaching:

After my first degree, I had other interests, my exposure to politics had created a greater focus on education of adults for the political process.

Jenny had a sense of dissatisfaction at about this same time but was unable to articulate it in definite terms. The question of whether they were "getting anywhere" surfaced for Sharie and Barbara who were of the same age as Jenny and Arlene, though they admitted that it had taken some time for the question to assume definitive shape. The perception that teaching lacked opportunity for personal growth and advancement was strong and pervasive. Sharie identified strong feelings in this regard:

There was the senior teacher post of course: more responsibility but not much more pay. Did I want to be a principal? No! (Sharie)

Even though I was a senior teacher, increasingly, I felt there was no where else to go; no scope for growth. (Barbara)

For Arlene and Al these feelings coincided with a loss of conviction that what they were doing was as crucial or useful as they had originally believed.

Political events in the country were impacting on the system; I wanted contact with minds but without the constraint of preparing them for the exam. (Al)

I found myself talking with them about themselves as persons, I was grappling without training, with their deeper adolescent concerns. I felt limited as a subject teacher with little hope of influencing decisions about how time should be spent. I didn't feel I was getting to the heart of the matter . . . whatever that was . . . (Arlene)

The stage described above appears to be one which does not of itself lead to a decision to terminate the teaching career. For some persons, it provided an impetus to identify personal development needs and to pursue training within the field. In some instances, the perception that the career had shortcomings was being reinforced or aggravated by coincidental circumstances in personal and family life. In the case of

Sharie, the beginning of personal dissatisfaction "was probably delayed by her husband's involvement in the same profession, which created the feeling of being in this thing together". Eventually, his departure and the subsequent large-scale exit of many peers began to create the feeling of being left behind:

I started to examine myself . . . to wonder if something might be wrong with me . . .

Stage 4 – Society's valuations and decision to leave

These valuations were evident in the financial rewards paid to teachers, as well as the physical resources, the teaching materials provided by the school, and the low regard in which teachers were now held. The sheer realities of the increasing cost of living during the seventies and early eighties, had provided what seemed to be a decisive blow against any inclination to weather the other storms which the teachers had been experiencing. The realization that remaining in the profession would not enable them to meet other responsibilities was just too much to tolerate:

I started teaching very young: my two children are at the university stage now; we are still in my mother's house; the salary just didn't allow me to come out . . . (Barbara)

Sharie confessed to feeling that with two young children she had a responsibility to play a stronger economic role than teaching was allowing. She recalled the anxiety she felt at the time, still showing great agitation about it:

Each month end I looked at my cheque and thought of the children, the home we wanted to build. I couldn't help . . . not even one cent! Something was being questioned in my very soul! . . .

No . . . with a wife and child it really was not going to work. . . I couldn't fool myself . . . (Colin)

I wanted my own economic base . . . teaching would not provide this . . . (Arlene)

The economic problem also manifested itself in several aspects of the overall classroom situation. A major recurrent theme was the concern amongst the teachers about the rapidly deteriorating physical conditions and resources, evidence of which I myself had found long after they had all moved on. For the teachers, the lack of acceptable conditions and resources was just further evidence that education was not priority at the national level. One crippling aspect of the whole situation was the evidence that nobody intended to put the resources into the schools. All the respondents were visibly angry as they described the staffroom, the noise, the dirt, the lack of resources which all worked together to convey "clear lack of importance placed by the society on education".

Physical conditions in the school represented only one of many manifestations of what respondents saw as a rapid decline between the seventies and eighties, in the regard for education and for teachers held in the wider society. Sharie made a clear comparison between her entry and the period preceding her departure:

> The teacher was highly regarded then, but just before I was leaving it was like a bad word. It was demoralizing to stand at the bus-stop waiting, knowing you are worth something, but realizing that the society just does not reflect this.

Arlene had become increasingly aware of pressure from outside, encouraging the feeling in her that she should have been doing better:

> After a while everybody greeted you with the same question, "Are you still in teaching?"

The dual experience of economic deprivation and loss of regard appeared to have a devastating effect on the self-esteem of the teachers, particularly as it related to their knowledge of what students were thinking about them. Colin recalled receiving serious advice from a former student:

> I met him on the street and he said, "But sir, Accounts is a good subject, you know. Why stay in teaching?"

Sharie's account revealed a much less positive encounter. She related incidents in which she was "deeply hurt and humiliated when former students returned to the school displaying superior attitudes to the very same teachers who had struggled to get them to learn something":

> I remember one particular boy . . . a real dunce! He came back driving this flashy car and he actually said to a teacher: "But sir, how you still in this place teaching? You don't have ambition?" I told myself then and there that such a thing must never happen to me!

Although an incident related by Barbara had occurred long after her departure and just a few months before our interview, she described the loss of respect for teachers with equally strong feelings:

> Recently, I read in the newspaper about a higgler who confronted a teacher regarding her child and said abusively that the money that the teacher earned was much less than what she "threw for partner"! I mean, there is just no respect. The children know it and they behave accordingly.

The breakdown in discipline and decreasing respect for teachers were associated concerns. The apparent lack of emphasis on education, accompanied by growing disrespect for teachers, seemed to account for some of the indiscipline amongst students.

> With the new type of children and the social attitudes, there wasn't any real chance of success. (Barbara)

> The teachers were demoralized; no respect, especially for the ladies; boys sat on the steps as the ladies tried to come down the stairs; they were always testing you, and not everyone realized that the shouting was not working. (Colin)

Another influence on these teachers' views of teaching were the attitudes and behaviour patterns of other teachers. Jenny believed that in spite of everything she might have been able to stay longer in the classroom had it not been for her gradual loss of confidence in the respectability of her peer group:

41

I knew it wasn't right for us to be looked down upon; but I came to feel that some of us deserved it; we didn't have the values, we weren't setting the example . . .

Arlene reflected on days which ended with her feeling that she needed contact with persons who could encourage positive feelings of worth in the face of the social evidence that teachers were losing ground in so many ways:

Sometimes, I wondered how we expected respect and success when our own behaviour was sometimes slovenly; chatting and laughing in the staffroom while students waited, teachers quarrelling with students as if they were all on the same level . . .

I didn't want this to rub off on me. I wanted to leave while I still had good feelings about teaching and after a while such feelings were being eroded. (Arlene)

Stage 5 – Conflict, guilt and departure

Despite the strength of the feelings expressed, the actual departure was not easy. All six teachers vacillated, even though intellectually and rationally their decisions had been made. This could be described as a somewhat "seasonal" vacillation based on typical events in the school calendar:

At mid-year you were preparing a group for the June exams, your focus is on them and you think you must see these through and then go . . . (Colin)

Each academic year I said this would be the last but then I got involved and wanted to see another set to graduation . . . (Barbara)

I kept saying, this is not the right time; it just can't be to any old job . . . (Sharie)

Definitely guilt; I asked myself what would happen if everyone left. I felt it was wrong to do something which would affect the boys when the conditions which I hated had not been of their making. (Arlene)

There was emotional conflict. I was the longest-serving member of the department and I was helping new teachers. I had some good prospects for the O levels and I couldn't think well of leaving them . . . (Colin)

For five of the six teachers, there appeared to be a need for a transitional experience to ease them out of the situation, rather than making a clean break:

I left before the exam and graduation; I knew that if I waited until the end of the school year I would again have been drawn in by the hope that I'd feel better after the summer and that next year would be better . . . (Barbara)

Yes, it was vital to leave before I started focusing on the fourth form because if I did I would start thinking I must stay until their exam! (Colin)

Some of the teachers in this study continued to teach long after they had made the decision to leave because of these feelings of guilt and conflict. These feelings are a reflection of their sense of commitment to the students and to the profession. And most of these six teachers subsequently chose careers which are related to education – adult literacy, human resource development, and training in industry. Some have decided to continue being a teacher by giving "extra lessons"; some claim that they will always be involved in education.

Although this is a study of only six teachers, it provides much insight into the rewards and satisfactions of teaching and sheds some light on the limits of teacher commitment. But there is a distinction between commitment to teaching and identifying proudly with the profession (Feiman-Nemser and Floden, 1986). In the end this was one of the main reasons why these teachers finally decided to leave – because they could no longer identify proudly with teaching. We see in the story of these teachers the importance of social forces, public valuation, ecological conditions at the workplace, and personal and family needs. We also see that the behaviour and decorum of fellow teachers as well as students can have a great effect on teacher satisfaction and their proud identification with the profession.

43

The six interviewees in this study represent a subgroup of teachers who were university trained, and who taught at the secondary level in an urban area during the 1970s and 1980s. There are other subgroups of teachers whose experiences and perspectives on teaching as a career are worth studying – elementary teachers, teachers without a university degree, rural teachers, unmarried teachers, and specialist teachers. A knowledge of their experiences and points of view will provide us a with a broader view of the rewards and satisfactions of teaching, as perceived by teachers in the 1990s and in the first decades of the twenty-first century. Such knowledge will also enable us to be more realistic in our plans to attract and retain teachers in the profession.

Students

Although teachers have a great deal of authority and power, students exercise much influence over what happens in classrooms. The teacher/student relationship is created as much by teachers – their caring, skill and regard for students – as it is by the students themselves and their perception of how the teacher regards them. Students are also significant in shaping the experience and identity of other students. A student's social self, and his or her self-concept and self-esteem, can be shaped by acceptance or rejection within the peer group. Most students have favourable attitudes toward their school and their teachers.

What is the experience of schooling like for students? What is it like to be compelled to go to a place where one is directed by others, where one has to follow rules and regulations? The disadvantages of school may be outweighed by its attractions which include meeting and chatting with friends, playing, engaging in sports and so on. In Jamaica, research on students' views of their school experience is contradictory. On the one hand, there is research which indicates that students like school, and look forward to going to school (Brock and Cammish, 1991; Evans, 1991). Some reasons which all-age and primary school students give for liking school are: they learn new things, they see and talk with their friends, they have helpful and caring teachers and they take part in sports and games (Brock and Cammish, 1991; Evans, 1991). A more recent study of secondary students from all types of schools presents a different picture. More than 95 percent of the students in that study stated that they did not like being in school, more than 85 percent felt that they did not belong in school and approximately 80 percent would have liked to be treated with more respect at school (Evans, 1998).

These results suggest that there is a negative side to school, as those who are familiar with schools are aware. Jackson (1968) described American classrooms as places where students have to contend with crowds, waiting for long periods of time, and with public evaluations such as rebukes and praise by the teacher. Students reported "the frightening or embarrassing experiences resulting from the actions of cruel and insensitive teachers and classmates" and "feelings of boredom arising from the meaninglessness of the assigned tasks" (p. 42). Okey and Cusick (1995) have shown that many American students suffer from class bullies, the exclusiveness of the class system, and the stigma of being seen as "dumb". Connell et al. (1982) found that working-class students in Australia have had "a mixture of good and bad moments; helpful teachers remembered with warmth, others with annoyance; often increasing boredom . . ." (p. 46). So each student has good and bad experiences and some students are more likely to have bad experiences than others. The nature of these experiences have much to do with the relationship with their peers, as well as with their teachers.

Students themselves engage in evaluation and self-evaluation of a social sort. They sometimes have to think about impression management, since evaluation of one's performance and hence, one's ability, is so public in classrooms. One's academic standing in a classroom is very significant. It helps to determine one's social standing in the classroom setting and may even be a major consideration when students select their friends. Students also have to establish some degree of social intimacy with other students. This is where many lasting friendships are formed. And they have to live with the power of the adults in the school. Students have to work when they are told to, even when they do not feel like it. They learn very soon the importance of conforming to rules and regulations; otherwise, they feel the harshness of the teacher's anger, or the sting of the strap.

Not all students experience school in the same way, and some students are more likely to feel positive about school than others. We have seen that there are different types of schools and that some schools do not have adequate resources and equipment. The general tone and the culture of the school will affect students' experiences and the sentiments that they form about schools. And it is reasonable to expect that younger students, such as those in the early grades of the primary and all-age school, will feel less ambivalent about school than older adolescents. There is evidence that teachers respond to students differently, depending on such factors as the student's ability, social class, race or colour, general demeanour in class, and gender. In Jamaica, it has been found that girls and those who are brown-skinned are more likely to be given more positive evaluations and to have more positive interactions with the teacher (Keith, 1976); those who are from poorer socioeconomic groups are also more likely to be placed in the low stream (Keith, 1976), and to be ridiculed and verbally abused by the teacher (Evans, 1998). Teachers also respond differently to girls and boys, as will be shown in a later chapter.

The student's academic ability is perhaps the most important defining characteristic determining how teachers, parents, and other students respond to him or her. The student's understanding, participation and performance in class are important indicators of whether that student is learning and provide positive reinforcement for the teacher's effort. It is also a source of the teacher's rewards and a parent's pride. On the other hand, the student who is slow to learn is a big challenge for the teacher and a source of worry and even frustration for the parent. Students who are not performing well in school usually know this only too well. They are reminded of this in almost every interaction with the teacher and often with other students. It appears that such students not only need and require more attention from the teacher, but the ways in which they seek that attention are not always appropriate. And there is evidence that when such students make demands on the teacher, they are interpreted differently from demands made by high-achieving students. Teachers therefore do not respond by providing the attention that the low ability student needs (Connell et al., 1982). And the effects can be severe and long-lasting. As Senior (1991: 54) has observed, "the wounds to one's self-esteem caused by not being able to learn in school are incalculable". Women interviewed in the WICP reported the devastating effect on them of not being able to keep up in class. And because the curriculum and the teaching methods did not allow for individual variation in ability or for individual attention, school became very punishing to the point where these girls often dropped out of school (Senior, 1991: 54–55). Women interviewed by Ford Smith reported similar experiences (Sistren, 1986). Although the women interviewed for the WICP went to school in the 1940s and 1950s, and those interviewed by Ford Smith went to school in the 1960s and 1970s, there is little evidence that the situation has changed. In an ongoing study, boys who have dropped out of school have also reported that one reason for dropping out was their inability to read, as well as the harsh, disrespectful, and insensitive treatment that they received from teachers (Miller, personal communication based on research in progress). Students who are poor performers or who are in the low stream are more likely to drop out than other students (Fine, 1986; Okey and Cusick, 1995).

Parents make important decisions about their children on the basis of academic ability. If a child is slow to learn, the parent may not expect the teacher to do much for him or her, and may even not bother to send the child to school. On the other hand, if the child shows promise and if the parents receive good reports from the teacher, parents are likely to make sacrifices for that child. In poorer families, this sacrifice may be at the expense of the less academically able child. The parents may lower expectations for the low-achieving child – and may not even hold teachers or the school accountable for learning. Seaga (1955), in his study of a rural Jamaican community in the 1950s, found that parents took their children's ability into account in their expectations of what the teacher could achieve.

In many ways, students are aided in their educational experience by the family background from which they come. Coleman (1988) has argued that family background can be analytically separated into financial, human, and social capital. While the financial capital provides the physical resources that can potentially aid the child's educational achievement – e.g., books to read and a place to do homework – the human capital in the form of the parents' education can contribute significantly to the child's intellectual development through the information passed on in conversations, and explanations provided on an ad hoc basis. It is, however, the social capital within the family that ultimately makes the difference. Social capital refers to the "strength of the relations between parents and child" (p. S110), and is a measure of the availability of the parents for the child. "Social capital within the family that gives the child access to the adult's human capital depends on the presence of the adults in the family and the attention given by the adults to the child" (p. S111). Parents therefore who are present and available for interacting in positive ways with the child make a difference to their children's education. It is therefore possible that a parent lacking in human capital can contribute more to a child's development and his or her academic achievement than one who is not. The social capital within the home can also make a difference in the personality of the child which can ultimately affect the way in which the child adapts to school and to the teacher. Social changes within the Jamaican society have led to highly differentiated experiences of family life for young people. These different family circumstances lead not only to differences in socialization practices in the home but in the social capital of the home and hence to the behaviours and personalities of students that teachers meet and contend with at school.

Some children are better able to establish good relations with the teacher and to adapt to the demands of school than others. The physical appearance and behaviour of the child (such as being well-mannered) can influence the teacher's reaction to children. As we have seen, the students' social class also has an important influence on the way the teacher interacts with students. Students from middle- and upper-middle-class families are more likely to be accepted by and to receive more attention from the teacher. Becker's (1984) study, carried out in the 1950s in the United States, in part helps us to understand why. Middle-class students are more likely to have the proper study habits, and appearance, and to comport themselves in ways of which the teacher approves. Students' race or, in the Jamaican context, their colour may also influence the teacher's response to students. There is some correlation between race/colour and social class which may in part explain why race and colour influence the teacher. But there are historical and social reasons why race and colour function as an important influence in face-to-face interactions in the society in general as well as in the schools. In Jamaica, for example, white or brown-skinned persons may be accorded more status in some social situations than persons who are black. The classroom is not isolated from wider social forces. This means that a student with high academic ability, who is from the middle classes and comports himself or herself well in class, is responded to positively by teachers and students alike. A poor student who is not so bright has a hard time of it. If that student misbehaves in class, the situation gets much worse.

It is likely also that there is more communication between the teacher and a parent from the middle and upper classes. Parents are differentially positioned in their interaction with the school and teachers know this. Parents from low socioeconomic groups are less likely to go to the school or to ask questions of the teacher. Parents from lower socioeconomic groups do not feel comfortable in schools and are often intimidated by teachers (Becker, 1984; Okey and Cusick, 1995). The suspiciousness of teachers on the part of Rural Ridge parents which Seaga found in the 1950s is still very common among parents of this socioeconomic group in

Jamaica. In a study of all-age schools, Evans (1988) found that parents and teacher rarely saw one another. Many of these teachers did not know the parents of their students, a situation which was accepted by parents and not viewed as extraordinary. On the other hand, parents who are more educated are more present in their children's school and often feel that they should be involved in their children's education, especially during the early years. Not all teachers react positively to this involvement on the part of parents. Some teachers see it as an intrusion in their professional responsibility, preferring instead that parents play a supportive role (Wells, 1998).

Given that academic ability is such an important factor in determining the teacher/student interaction and the quality of the learning experience, placement in a class streamed by ability will make a big difference to the kind of experience which students have in classrooms and the curriculum which they are required to learn. The majority of students who are placed in the low streams come from poor or working-class families. The reasons why this is so, and the experience and effects of streaming will be explored in Chapter 5. Gender also plays a significant part in structuring the schooling experience at both the primary and secondary levels, as we have seen. The dynamics of gender and the different experiences of boys and girls in schools will be discussed in Chapter 6.

It must be recognized, however, that students do not come into a classroom and misbehave or get ignored or ridiculed solely on the basis of their social class, colour or gender. The students' behaviour and the ways in which others respond to that behaviour form part of the dynamics of classroom interaction. Students' behaviour, others' reaction to it, the impressions which are created or the meanings ascribed to what is said and done, explain in part why some students decide to make an effort to participate or to please the teacher, while others choose not to. The young child goes to school with much pleasurable anticipation. Some of these students come to like the teacher, understand what is taught and feel good about school. Others, for various reasons, do not participate, develop a dislike for school and eventually drop out or remain in school but are detached. Students' achievement, performance or propensity to conform or misbehave are socially constructed within the classroom itself. Each student responds to the teacher – what is said and done, the tone of voice, and the fairness and equality of the interaction. Each student makes an assessment of the teacher and his or her competence, caring, and fairness. Students have expectations of the teacher. Here are the views of students

49

from around the world on what they expect from teachers:

> You need to be kind trusting and friendly to me . . . you must listen and understand us all . . . never lose your temper or ignore us . . . I like a smile and a kind word.

> A good teacher should treat all pupils like his own children. He should answer all questions even if they are stupid.

> A good teacher does not have any favourites and does not separate the poor from the rich and the not-so-intelligent from the intelligent.

> A good teacher must understand every child's needs and try to bring out the best in each pupil.

> (UNESCO, 1996)

Students develop an attitude toward school and school work based in part on their perceptions of the teacher's behaviour, but also on how well they seem to be doing in school and how their classmates respond to them. They also respond to being in an environment where there is acceptance, trust, caring, and where they can have a feeling of safety and satisfaction. But as we have seen, some teachers have difficulty in establishing that caring and warmth with some students and in particular students who are labelled slow or who are placed in the low stream. In Chapter 5, where issues of streaming are examined, we shall hear the voices of low stream students regarding how they perceive teachers' and parents' expectations, and the pain which low expectations bring. These expectations are often influenced by the students' low academic ability, as well as students' social class or "background".

Teachers, Students and the Use of Authority

It is in the school setting that teachers learn what it means to teach, learn about students and how to interact with them, and learn to understand and use authority. The role of the teacher has inherent in it some degree of formal or institutional authority. The school as an institution and, by extension, the wider society accords this formal authority to the teacher. This authority is linked to the purposes of the institution which are to help students learn worthwhile things, and to develop in appropriate ways. Although the college programme provides the required knowledge and skills and may have introduced the student teacher to the concept of teacher authority and power, it is at the work setting, in specific interactions with students, that the teacher comes to understand the nature, limits, and responsibilities of authority and power. The practice of teaching requires this authority on the part of the teacher. If students are to learn, if they are to pay attention and behave appropriately in a group situation, there must be rules for behaviour and some kind of social control. Decisions about such rules and control are within the teacher's authority, and he or she may make these decisions in an arbitrary, authoritarian or democratic manner. One may get students to do one's bidding by giving orders, by setting expectations or creating a desire among students to act in certain ways.

Teachers create the social environment of the classroom and formulate and insist on the standards of behaviour that shape how students and teachers interact with one another. They set the tone of the classroom, and influence students by the example of their behaviour. They decide what is to be discussed and what is worth talking about. They make evaluations of students' contributions to classroom discussion and in addition evaluate students' behaviour. They pose questions and give explanations that not only determine the level of discourse but whether students leave that class with a clearer understanding of the subject matter or with misconceptions. Teachers indeed have the power of creating the self-fulfilling prophecy – influencing students to think and act in ways which conform with their expectations. They may also affect the students' desire to stay in school or to drop out. A study of drop-outs in the United States showed that the majority of the drop-outs interviewed saw themselves as "victims of unfeeling teachers, oppressive administrators and bullying classmates" (Okey and Cusick, 1995: 257). But teachers do not often recognize their power over students, neither do they always have a clear understanding of their authority and its institutional bases.

It may be that a teacher's conception of his or her authority and power grows and develops over time. McLaughlin (1994) describes the evolution of his understanding of his authority from student teaching to university teaching. As a student teacher, he believed that knowing the subject matter and having humane intentions toward students would suffice as a teacher. But students' misbehaviours, the lack of order in the activities planned and his anger at students' failure to conform to his expectations

51

made him realize that his "authority as a teacher was predicated on how I related personally to students – and their caring for me" (p. 60). At the same time he realized that he had to have a workable plan for enabling students to cooperate (p. 60). He began to learn the tensions between caring and asserting power. As a graduate student, he began to learn that power was not something he possessed but was the "capability to act" – fostered by an understanding of his role and the relationships he nurtured. His understanding of the nature of authority and power continued to grow as a university teacher when be became familiar with the literature on power. He came to realize that authority is a grant to exercise power, but "the students must confer authority if the teacher is to succeed in creating an environment conducive to learning" (p. 62).

The power of the teacher extends to students' learning. Some would say "it all depends on the teacher" as parents who listen to stories from school or pay attention to the reputation of individual teachers may come to believe. It is true that the individual teacher with commitment, a caring attitude to children, and an understanding of how to bring about learning can make a big difference. This is where teachers' personal qualities, skills, and understanding of what it means to teach can make a difference to what and how much students learn. But as Goodlad (1984) points out, this can only be done under the right conditions, which include availability of resources such as teaching/learning materials, administrative and parental support, among others. Hence, we cannot blame teachers for student outcomes without taking into account the resources available and without considering students' commitment to learning. Personal and biographical factors also influence the teacher's ability to create effective learning experiences and provide a caring environment for students. According to Greene (1991), it all comes down to what the teacher is trying to bring into being, and what teaching means for that teacher. Teaching must be endowed with some meaning, whether it is focused on being caring to students, on the social development of students, or on the rigours of teaching an academic discipline. This concern and this meaning make the teacher existentially present to students and how they are learning. It makes the teacher reflect on appropriate means and ends in teaching. But Greene admits that teachers, faced with pressures, can easily become uninvolved, resigned or alienated.

The teacher also has a critical role to play in kindling students' interest and in orienting them to the structure and the concepts of a discipline or area of study. This role of opening the door to learning subject matter is particularly acute for students whose families do not regularly engage with these ideas. Mike Rose, an American who spent many years helping students from immigrant or working-class families to learn to write in English at the level required of the university, reflects on this important function of the teacher. For him, opening this door to learning includes establishing a relationship, taking the time to know and understand the student's difficulties, and being able to explain, translate and in some way help the student to cross that bridge of understanding. "[In teaching], you didn't just work with words or a chronicle of dates or facts . . . You wooed kids with these things, invited a relationship of sorts . . . Knowledge gained its meaning at least initially, through a touch on the shoulder, through a conversation . . ." (Rose, 1989: 102). In his writing programme at the University of California at Los Angeles (UCLA), designed mainly for students from immigrant and working-class homes, Rose describes the difference that this approach to teaching made to students who were once labelled slow or remedial. Once someone had taken the time to explain basic terms, to make connections to a network of ideas, such students could become part of the conversation from which they had previously been excluded.

While the teacher has a responsibility to establish a relationship with students, maintaining this relationship represents major challenges for some teachers. As some educational sociologists have pointed out, there is an inherent conflict between the teacher role and the student role. Willis (1978) refers to this relationship as one between potential contenders for supremacy. To students, teachers represent the adult group which enforces rules and regulations. At times, the teacher has to make students work against their will. Dominance and control therefore become part of the teacher/student relationship; and as we have seen, the formal authority of the teacher legitimizes this dominance and control. But as Rose (1989), McLaughlin (1994) and others have discovered, the teacher has to develop an ongoing relationship with the student – one that makes the student want to do his or her bidding. One of the first lessons that many young and inexperienced teachers learn is the necessity to exercise this control and authority, as well as to joke, laugh, and show caring for students. This necessity to dominate and at the same time to develop and maintain a good relationship with one's students is one example of the dual, conflicting demands which teaching makes on teachers. Teachers have to think of the good of all the students in their care – the universal requirements – and at the same time, think of the needs of that one child who needs his or her attention. These demands create dilemmas, which are a result of conflicting goals, of the tensions between ideals and practical constraints, and between one's values and institutional purposes (Lortie, 1975; Jackson, 1986).

At the same time, however, teachers are dependent on students for the results of their work. For although it is the students' duty to learn, it is the teacher's responsibility to facilitate that learning. Schools and colleagues judge teachers on the basis of students' outcomes. So combined with the teacher's authority and power is the teacher's dependence on students. It is this combination of authority, power, and dependence on those who are institutionally subordinate which makes the teacher so vulnerable and which makes the teacher/student relationship problematic. Herein lies the "paradox of authority and vulnerability" (Metz, 1993: 108). "To be dependent on clients who are children for the accomplishment of one's own success is both technologically paradoxical and socially demeaning" (Metz, 1993: 105). But demeaning as it is, it is a lesson that all teachers must learn. Teachers who are both loved and are effective have learned this lesson very well. New teachers fail to learn this crucial lesson at their peril. They cannot rely on skills and techniques of classroom management alone. A relationship has to be established with students. For the teacher can obtain his or her psychic rewards and the results which she is paid to achieve only through the cooperation and acquiescence of students. The teacher's ability to gain students' active attention, and to obtain their assent or cooperation in learning tasks is crucial in teaching. To make learning happen, and especially to transform and develop the thinking of another person, a teacher must have the student's cooperation. Cooperation requires some degree of mutuality and respect. It is this requirement of mutuality, trust, and respect which makes it difficult for some teachers to obtain the cooperation which they need. They may acknowledge students' subordinate role and their dependence on the teacher's knowledge and authority, but they may not recognize their own obligation to make students want to participate in learning. Many teachers find it easier to accord this mutuality and respect to some children than others. This "socially demeaning" position of the teacher may present even more of a challenge when the students are different in some way — for example, being of another race or ethnic group or of a lower socioeconomic class.

One of the earliest ethnographic studies of teachers and their work rewards was done in the 1950s by Becker (1984), who studied public school teachers in the city of Chicago. The teachers in his study had a model of the ideal pupil and judged students on the basis of their conformity with or divergence from this model. Becker found that teachers made class-based distinctions among students, judging them on their appearance, their language, and their willingness to be disciplined. "Slum" children caused many of the middle-class teachers much distress, a fact which made Becker point to the "differences in the educational opportunities available to children of various social classes" (1984: 98). Since Becker's study, many researchers in the United States and Great Britain have come to similar conclusions regarding the teacher's relationship and effectiveness with children who are different with respect to class, race, gender, ethnic group, and nationality (e.g., McDermott, 1977; Mac an Ghaill, 1994; Sewell, 1999)

This fundamental and inescapable characteristic of teaching – depending on students whom one has to direct and control – becomes acute when the students are adolescents. For at this stage of their development, students want to test the limits of authority and are loath to accord much importance to what adults say. When students see little value in education or schooling, or when the social identity which is in formation is at odds with the requirements of schooling, the teacher's job is more difficult. In her study of eight high schools in the United States, Metz (1993) has illustrated the problematic character of teachers' authority over high school students, especially those from poor neighbourhoods who did not plan to attend college. Such students come to school sceptical about the value of schooling and aware that in all likelihood, they will not be proceeding beyond high school. In her observational study, Metz found that students often responded to teaching by showing boredom, chatting in class, flouting school rules, and in general engaging in misbehaviours in class.

Metz also observed that when students responded in this fashion to teachers' efforts to teach them, teachers lost their self-confidence and commitment and had a range of emotions ranging from frustration and anger, to cynicism and resignation. Her study revealed how classroom processes – what students do and how they respond to teaching – can have an impact on teachers' attitude to their work and ultimately on their job satisfaction. Teachers do depend on their students for success, for evidence of that success and for the rewards which teaching brings. Very often, these rewards come in the form of the spectacular case or the "gratifying graduate", but in the short term, it may also be more objective information such as examination results, or evidence of student interest (Lortie, 1975). When students cannot or will not provide these rewards – i.e., evidence of the effects of what they do – teachers gain little satisfaction from their work and may in fact come to dislike the work and the students. On the other hand, as many teachers have attested, when the students demonstrate understanding, when they achieve, when indeed the teacher can recognize the results of his or her work, there is no greater reward or sense of satisfaction (Lortie, 1975; Goodlad, 1984). Such evidence is not always immediately available or easily obtained.

A recent study by Brown (1997) shows the effect that the absence of such rewards can have on teachers. In this study, we see an example of the breakdown of the teacher's authority because of the poor relation which existed between teachers and students. These students have decided to withdraw their cooperation in learning because of what they see as an absence of caring and trust on the part of teachers, the failure of teachers to believe in and respect them, and to attend to the school's major task – getting students to learn. It also reveals the cyclical relationship between teachers' commitment and caring, students' ability, students' (mis)behaviour, teachers' sense of satisfaction, their resulting relationship with students, students' respect for teachers, and their willingness to engage in learning.

Brown's study shows the process by which the relationship between the teacher and student breaks down, and teachers lose their commitment to achieving educational goals for a group of students, and students lose their respect for teachers. But the students in Form 3Q (a pseudonym) engaged in misbehaviours only with certain teachers and subjects. With two of their teachers, students paid attention and conformed to classroom rules, even when they found the subject matter difficult. Observation of the classes where teachers were listened to and respected revealed that these teachers had clear expectations for student behaviour, communicated these expectations, and showed that they expected students to conform to these expectations. But in addition, the teachers were willing to respond to students' needs and requests for help. Above all, students themselves had seen that their academic performance had improved in the subjects taught by these teachers. Students were willing to be controlled by such teachers – even with the use of corporal punishment – "because it was for their own good".

With all the other teachers of this form, however, the misbehaviour of students had become the core of the teacher/student relationship. When students challenged the teachers' authority and experienced problems in learning, these teachers' responses ranged from resignation and frustration to disdain, contempt, and hostility. Some adopted an approach which combined punitiveness and coercion with disrespect. It was clear that these teachers had low expectations for these students and were not prepared to find out or address their learning needs. The students, on the other hand, recognized that these teachers did not care about them and that they were not fulfilling their professional obligations. Teachers, it was felt, no longer had a commitment to them as students and this recognition created an even further divide between teacher and student. We see in this study that students respect teachers when they, the teachers, exercise some form of authority over students in the service of learning. Problems and conflicts arise between teacher and students when students perceive that the teacher is defaulting on this basic obligation.

The study was an ethnographic study of a class of low stream third form students at a secondary high school for boys. The researcher carried out observations and interviews over a period of two months. The aim was to discover the reasons why students misbehaved and were disruptive in class. In the following excerpts, we see descriptions of students' behaviour in class, teachers' and students' perceptions of these behaviours, and the reasons students give for misbehaviour. Disruptive behaviour was defined as behaviour that works against effective teaching· and learning and included noise making, disobedience to teachers, lateness and absenteeism, and disorderliness.

The extract below from Brown's study reveals the many ways in which the teacher's authority can be eroded.

> There are approximately forty-three students in Form 3Q (a pseudonym), a low stream class in a secondary high school for boys in a large urban area. Many of these students had entered the school in second form in a special sports recruitment programme. The walls of the rooms are somewhat defaced and on the display board to the back of the room one sees evidence of graffiti that students have written. Quite a few of these represent the aliases by which students are called by both teachers and peers. There was no evidence of charts or visual aids being used in the classroom. There was a strong reliance on textbooks by the teachers with the chalkboard used to display information. Students are required to be on time and seated before the teacher arrives. They are also expected to have their books and other materials on their desk and be prepared to participate in class. School

rules do not allow talking among students, shouting in class or leaving the class without permission. However, students routinely disregarded these rules.

Misbehaviours observed during my observations included students walking in and out of classes, shouting while the teacher was present, throwing things across the room, being disrespectful to teachers, sleeping in class, looking at another's work during a test, playing games in class, and standing at the classroom door while the teacher was present. Students also absented themselves from classes fairly regularly. Students were able to recognize when their behaviour was disruptive. They were also aware that their behaviour disrupted teaching activities and prevented other students from learning. They knew what disruptive behaviour was, defining it as: speaking out of turn during a lesson; not obeying the teacher; going around in the classroom and doing what you are not supposed to be doing; walking in and out of classroom without permission; shouting in class; giving trouble, fighting, interrupting the lesson, and distracting the students.

Despite this general consensus, I also noticed that students were not disruptive during every lesson. Much depended on which lesson and which teacher. During lessons taught by two teachers particularly, these students behaved themselves well. They sat in their seats and there was no excessive talking or shouting across the room. The teacher was able to conduct the lesson and moved around the class to give individual attention. Watching these students during these lessons it seemed that they behaved themselves because they knew that the teacher expected them to behave. The vignette below gives a synopsis of how students behaved in one of these classes.

On entering the classroom the teacher greeted the students and then said to them: "Students tidy up your classroom. You are doing a test today and I won't hand out the test papers until you settle down." There was a buzz of activity as students rearranged furniture and retrieved materials from their desks and bags to write their tests. After a few minutes, the class settled down and students received their test papers. I noticed the difference in attitude of one student who was extremely disruptive during other lessons. Whereas he was shouting and making much noise earlier, he was well settled now.

On a second occasion, I noted that the students behaved in a similar manner with this teacher. As soon as he entered the classroom, students sat down and started paying attention. As the teacher began to discuss the homework most of them informed him that they had found it difficult and therefore had not done it. The teacher then reviewed the work by showing solutions on the chalkboard and then asked students to try and find solutions to those not done. While students worked he walked around and monitored them. Students who wanted assistance raised their hands and indicated that they needed help. It seemed that these students knew that the teacher expected them to behave themselves. Later, the teacher discussed the solution to the task that he had assigned them. It was interesting to watch these students when they realized that their solutions were correct. They smiled with one another and were quite enthusiastic in their reactions. There was no evidence of the teacher employing corporal punishment in order to maintain discipline.

Students and teachers agreed that the two teachers were the only ones who could control the students. The reason was they employed corporal punishment as a means of maintaining discipline over these students. While students believed that most teachers could not control the boys and it was the students who had the "upper hand", they saw these two teachers as the exception. Students' perspective on discipline, and students' behaviour changed when they spoke of these two teachers. Students said they needed to be controlled because it was for their own good. And they had observed that their academic performance improved with these two teachers.

With other teachers, however, their behaviour was quite different. The following is an extract from field notes taken during a lesson taught by another teacher:

> *The boys are extremely noisy and although the teacher is present he is being ignored by his students. One boy shouts to the teacher, "Sir, you teach fourth form?" The teacher responds, "Buoy, wha you nuh shut up." The teacher then reminds the students that he is writing a test on the chalkboard. While the teacher is still writing, the boys have their notebooks opened and most of them are still talking to their peers . . . There are twenty students present. Suddenly the teacher shouts "you have a zero" and then records the zero. To this the student responds "Sir, yu caan do dat." Another student*

shouts to me "miss yu know anything about _____ (subject)? Can you help me, miss?" The teacher responds "Shut up" and so I (researcher) do not have to reply to the student. Another student shouts, "Sir, we don't understand." Yet another student shouted "Sir _____ (name of subject) don't make sense" . . . After a while, another asked the question "Sir which class does _____ (subject) well?" The teacher replies "Not this class." (The student makes a comment which is inaudible.) The teacher's response is "Not everyone is as handicapped as you." A few minutes later, one student walks out without seeking permission from the teacher.

When students failed to understand what was being taught, they became frustrated and quickly found ways to express their frustration. On one occasion during a test, several students complained about the difficulty of the work. After the teacher had written the test questions on the chalkboard, students began asking him to explain what certain questions meant and what information was needed to answer the question. After about ten minutes of just sitting and not attempting to do anything one boy shouted, "Sir give us an open book test; this is too difficult." Another one shouted, "Sir you did not teach us that." The class became extremely restless and some students started looking in their neighbours' answer sheets.

Some teachers no longer responded to the students' behaviour, since these students had now been labelled as uncontrollable. This attitude on the part of some teachers is reflected in the following exchange recorded in my field notes:

As I sat observing a lesson, the students were very unsettled and would not give much attention to what the teacher was saying. The teacher stood during most of the session and watched the students without saying anything. At the end of the class, I went over to the teacher to discuss what happened. To which he said "me not going to kill myself". The teacher, it appeared, was resigned to the situation and was no longer willing to exert himself to exercise control.

Teachers' discussions or conversations with students usually related to academic work. But whether the teacher was admonishing, informing, or correcting, the tone was often hostile, uncaring, sarcastic or disrespectful. The following exchanges were overheard in the classroom. A teacher is informing students about expectations for fourth form.

This term is crucial. This term you are going to prove to yourselves and your teachers that you can do certain subjects in fourth form. Nobody will be allowed to do certain subjects if the teacher says no. You have one last time to make up. God help you. If you don't make it now ask God to take you because the rest of your life will be a joke.

A teacher is scolding the student:

Wake up. You never sleep last night. I never sleep either but you gwine tan up today.

The teacher below is speaking to a student who is misbehaving:

Boy shut your mouth before I take chalk and mark you in your face.

Teachers' indifference to students is reflected in their lowered expectations for students' academic work and achievement. One teacher could not recall the last time she gave homework since no one did it. When the class did not do an assignment this teacher responded thus:

Nobody has done the homework. Let me remind you that the other classes have finished the unit. If you want to lag behind, that's your business.

The teachers sometimes punished students by refusing to award them grades for work done. The entire class can be punished by being given a zero because of the behaviour of one child. Students strongly objected to this practice.

To find out why students misbehaved in class, I conducted an in-depth interview and had informal conversations with both teachers and students. Students had various perspectives on this issue, ranging from students' desire for attention to lack of interest in the subject to difficulty in understanding the subject. The following are the views of the students.

Because nobody not paying them any attention. They try to get other students in trouble because they seek the teacher's attention.

They try to get other students in trouble because they want to get the attention of the teacher. They throw things around the class and this often leads into a fight. This is how one broke out this morning. The teacher gave him some handouts to give out but he did not want to share it with anybody.

Class boring miss.

Because the work is difficult sometimes the teacher is teaching and the students do not understand so they make a lot of noise so that those of us who are understanding cannot learn.

All the students with whom I spoke believed that the teachers did not care about them or about teaching. The following comments were made by students during our interview:

Miss, right now the teachers do not care about us, I don't think they can say anything good about this form. This makes me feel sad because I am a part of this class. If the teachers are talking about what a boy has done instead of calling the boy by name they just say (name of class).

I think some of the teachers don't care about us. It's like you mind you own business and I mind mine. For example, when teacher X has class with us he make us stand up a long time when we have a single session. After that he sits down and take a long time to mark the register. And after this it is just time for lunch.

Students felt that they had ability and should do well. What they needed was for teachers to motivate them and help them to achieve their goals. This in their view was not happening.

Another reason which students gave for their disruptive behaviour is their lack of interest in the subject and their dislike of the teacher. This is how one student explained it:

Some students skip lessons because certain classes (i.e., subjects) they do not like and are not interested in and so they do not come to class. They prefer to play marble.

The teachers had a slightly different perspective on the problem. All the teachers with whom I spoke agreed that the students in Form 3Q had some difficulty coping academically, and this influenced their behaviour. Being disruptive was one way of expressing their frustration. They felt that the students did not have a sense of purpose in being at school and as such, were only going through the routine. Students were attending school because they did not have a choice. Therefore, they came not with the intention of learning but to waste time. Since they did not study, and did not do homework, they would not do well academically. At the same time, however, some teachers have lessened their control and no longer used their authority. This teacher had this to say when asked what one could do to address the students' behaviour.

I think maybe we should get rid of the whole of them. I have never really thought of helping them to solve the problem. I just want to get rid of them where I don't have to teach them anymore. I just started teaching them in January and I don't want to teach them in fourth form. They waste time and everything is on you the teacher. The teacher gets all the blame.

The relationship between students and the majority of teachers in this form had deteriorated badly. There was mutual disrespect between teachers and students with teachers no longer willing to make the effort to try and build a relationship with students which would lead to a healthy classroom climate. Teachers did not have a high expectation of these students as many felt that they had no sense of purpose and school was just a place for them to engage in their "extra-curricular activities". Students, on the other hand, were very disappointed in their teachers as many felt that the teachers no longer cared about their welfare.

The research by Brown provides examples of the many demands and dilemmas facing the teacher today. The teacher has to exercise some degree of control and dominance over students in order to get them to engage in learning activities which may not interest them. To engage in these learning activities, students must not only attend to the academic or curricular demands but conform to the rules for behaviour in that class. The conduct of teaching/learning activities requires some minimal conformity to rules of behaviour. Teachers soon learn that any incipient misbehaviour or challenge to authority must be nipped in the bud, since students react to the behaviour of other students, as well as to the teacher's reaction to that behaviour. But such control without a moral basis becomes counterproductive. Brown's study shows that students are willing to be controlled, "for their own good", if teachers fulfil their side of the teaching/learning contract. But when control and dominance are carried out without this counter-responsibility on the part of the teacher and carried out without a sense of caring, students do not respond to being controlled.

The study also highlights the delicate nature of teacher authority. Although the teacher's formal authority is based on the institutional purpose of the school, to get students to learn and develop in worthwhile ways, the teacher's personal authority is based on the communication of expectations and a personal relationship with the students, or as McLaughlin (1994) discovered after many years of teaching, "how I relate personally to students and their caring for me". In this study, we also see the problems faced by teachers when they try to teach students who have been labelled "slow" or "remedial", or of low ability or in the low stream. These students do not easily experience the intrinsic rewards of learning and usually have difficulty in understanding and doing academic work. Because such students continually receive messages about their academic incompetence and other personal inadequacies, and because they often experience problems in learning, it is difficult for them to experience the intrinsic rewards of education or to envisage the benefits which such education brings. They therefore lack any immediate incentive to acquiesce to the teacher's demands for work. Teachers of students of low ability or those in the low stream therefore have to exercise a greater amount of coercion and control to get such students to work (Metz, 1978). If, however, this coercion is done without a sense of caring and a respectful and caring teacher/student relationship, as illustrated in this study, the teacher becomes and is seen as a bully.

This study also provides an example of the reduced access to knowledge and learning for those students assigned to a low stream – an issue that will be examined in more detail in Chapter 5. In this study, teachers did not make allowances or adjustments for the low ability students. Rarely were their needs addressed through special methods or materials which would address their learning needs. As in most secondary schools in Jamaica, the teachers relied heavily on the lecture method regardless of the ability level or needs of students. Ironically, the very students who needed special help were denied special learning experiences and the use of special equipment or resources because they were considered too slow to use them. The study also demonstrates the ways in which the curriculum and pedagogy influence students' interest and engagement in learning activities, and the fact that discipline cannot be separated from issues of streaming and pedagogy. These were working-class boys in a low stream, expected to learn little bits of knowledge unrelated to anything in their life from teachers with low expectations for them and obviously unwilling to establish a respectful relationship with them. Students resisted this in the only way they could – by withholding their cooperation. The issue of the curriculum, pedagogy, and the challenge of engaging working-class boys in learning will be further explored in the next chapter.

The public discourse on "discipline" or students' misbehaviour in Jamaican schools usually focuses on standards for behaviour and the control of students. Rarely does it make mention of the influence of the teacher/student relationship on students' behaviour or feelings about school. The student/teacher relationship – the expectations set, the caring demonstrated, and the climate created in a classroom – forms the basis for any control which the teacher has to exercise. It also forms the basis of trust. Such trust is critical to achieving learning and conforming behaviour. As Erickson (1987: 344) states, "learning what is deliberately taught can be seen as a form of political assent . . . Assent to the exercise of authority involves trust that its exercise will be benign . . . In the end, it is the student who by cooperating decides to grant the teacher control, an act that requires trust." These considerations must become part of the discourse on teaching, learning and "discipline" in our schools. At a time of immense social change, the role and obligations of the teacher and the nature of the curriculum must also be a part of that discourse.

It is within the context of the teacher/student relationship, the sentiments which students and teachers develop for one another, and the dynamics of classroom interaction, that the school carries out its various tasks which serve to socialize young people, to develop character, and to pass on knowledge, skills, and cultural values. The teacher's and the students' valuations are part of this environment; they influence students' participation in learning as well as their satisfaction with school. The teacher/student relationship is structured around the curriculum — the knowledge, skills, and attitudes that a society deems important for its young people to learn. This will be discussed in the next chapter.

4

The Curriculum and Teaching
What Schools and Classrooms Teach and How It Is Taught

In order to carry out its mission of educating its young, schools develop curricula that reflect some desired end points and that are appropriate for specific age groups. Some countries have centralized curricula wherein a central body, usually the Ministry of Education, determines what should be taught and transmits this information to the schools in the form of curricula and curriculum guides. In some countries, individual schools are free to develop their own curricula. In the United States, for example, individual schools are able to offer subjects and topics that they consider appropriate for the students who attend their schools and may do so at a level or standard that differs from that in other schools. While this affords some autonomy and freedom to the individual school, there is also the risk of schools offering a curriculum that is "watered down" or does not live up to acceptable standards. This charge has been levelled at some schools whose students are African American or who belong to immigrant populations (Oakes, 1985; Darling-Hammond, 1995). On the other hand, when a curriculum is centrally organized, the content or topics may not be wholly relevant to a particular community and local teachers have to be

67

able and willing and adapt the curriculum to local circumstances.

In Jamaica, curricula for Grades 1 to 9 are centrally planned by the MOEC. The curriculum guides for Grades 1 to 6 (primary) and Grades 7 to 9 (lower secondary) constitute the formal or explicit curriculum of all the public schools in Jamaica. At the higher levels of secondary education, Grades 10 to 11 and Sixth Form, the curriculum is determined by the content of the regional and external examinations that students sit such as the CXC examinations or the General Certificate of Education (GCE) Advanced level examinations, or by the national examinations such as the Secondary Schools Certificate (SSC) and the Jamaica High School Certificate (JHSC) examinations. The formal curriculum includes all the courses offered by the schools, the topics for these courses, the content in books, the teaching materials that teachers use, the emphases that the teacher takes in teaching, the guidelines given in preparing for tests, the actual tests that students take and so on.

The new curriculum developed under the auspices of PEIP has an integrated curriculum at Grades 1 to 3 and a more subject-based curriculum at Grades 4 to 6. An integrated curriculum means that lessons are taught around a certain theme, such as My Community, and within the exploration of that theme, numeracy, literacy, skills and scientific concepts are developed. This is in contrast to the subject-based approach in which subjects such as Mathematics or Science are taught separately. At the Grades 4 to 6 levels, the subjects are: Language Arts, Mathematics, Science, Social Studies, Religious Education, Drama, Visual Arts, Music and Physical Education (MOEC, 1999b). At the lower secondary level (Grades 7 to 9), the curriculum developed under the ROSE programme is also integrated, but within the traditional subject areas of Language Arts, Mathematics, Science, and Social Studies. In addition, there is a new subject called Resource and Technology that integrates the visual arts, product design and development, home and family management, agriculture and the environment, and resource management. Career Education is infused into all subject areas so that students can make decisions about careers linked to their interests and skills. The Grades 7 to 9 curriculum strongly recommends that collaborative learning principles be adopted in the teaching of the Grades 7 to 9 curriculum. This means that students are expected to collaborate in doing research, in helping and discussing the materials, and in making presentations to the class. In this way, it is expected that students will learn a degree of self-confidence (MOEC, 1993).

At the senior secondary level (Grades 10 to 11), there are now different types of secondary education offered to Jamaican students. This depends to some extent on the type of school one attends. But there are differences in options within each type of school as well. Secondary high schools offer mainly an academic curriculum as well as a mixed academic and technical/vocational curriculum. Thus, they teach mainly academic subjects such as History, Geography, and English with some technical and vocational subjects. Comprehensive high schools do the same, although some may place more or equal emphasis on the technical and vocational as well as on the academic. The technical high schools offer a similar mix, but with more emphasis on the technical and vocational subjects.

The majority of Grade 11 students now take the CXC examination which now offers examinations in sixty subjects. Schools that enter students for the CXC exam are guided by the syllabus developed by that body. Because this examination is a prerequisite for entry to the tertiary level, this upper secondary curriculum is to a great extent influenced by what is offered at the tertiary level. This is particularly so in the "academic" subjects such as History, Science, Mathematics, and Geography. In other words, the secondary academic curriculum seeks to prepare students for those subjects offered at the tertiary level of education. The CXC certificate also serves as a qualification for certain clerical and accounting jobs. In this way, the schools have become an important site for students to get the credentials that have become so necessary in today's society. However, with the downturn in the economy, the link between credentials and job opportunities is now greatly weakened. Young people with some high school education are as likely to be employed as those with a primary education (Anderson, 1997). As a result many young people may not necessarily see schooling as necessary for making it in life.

Not all students at the upper secondary level take the CXC examinations. The national locally administered examination, the SSC, is also available. It does not provide access to the tertiary level but is acceptable for entrance to some clerical jobs in the workplace. Language Arts, Science, Mathematics, and Social Studies are the only four "academic" subjects offered in this examination, but the content level is not the same as that of the CXC. Other technical/vocational subjects such as Auto Mechanics, Carpentry, and Shorthand are also offered in the SSC. Students who take these technical/vocational subjects receive the National Vocational Qualification of Jamaica (NVQJ) certificate. Many schools offer the SSC examination for those Grade 11 students who teachers think are not performing at the level of the CXC or who are unable to pay the fairly high fees required to sit the CXC and other external examinations. A sizeable proportion of secondary students, therefore, are offered a curriculum that curtails their access to tertiary education. Many of these students are from the working class and are to be found in the low streams or special "SSC" streams in the new secondary and comprehensive high schools, or schools newly upgraded to high school status.

When a curriculum is organized around bodies of knowledge that are tested in order to serve as credentials for access to further education, it takes on certain characteristics. Connell (1985) has referred to such a curriculum as the "competitive academic curriculum". This curriculum is, in his view, "hegemonic", not because it is the only curriculum in the school but because

> it has pride of place in the schools, it dominates most people's ideas of what real learning is about; its logic has the most powerful influence on the organization of the school, and of the education system generally; and it is able to marginalise or subordinate the other curricula that are present . . . (p. 87)

The competitive academic curriculum has the following features: the knowledge to be taught is derived from university-based disciplines like History, Mathematics, and Geography. Second, the knowledge is organized hierarchically, from less to more difficult or from basic principles to later elaborations. Third, the teaching is basically transfer teaching. What the teacher knows about the body of knowledge is transferred to the mind of the pupil. This means that the whole course of learning can be laid down in advance. Fourth, student learning is organized as appropriation of bits of knowledge, i.e., they learn in parallel not in a joint or collaborative manner. And when this learning is assessed, it is how much each student knows individually of these bits of knowledge – not what they can do with it collectively. Fifth, the knowledge learned is regularly tested to determine who has learned most and least. The results of these tests are publicly certified and used to determine entry to further education and to the job market. Many teachers, it seems, are attached to and uncritical of this curriculum because they have been products of it. The curriculum therefore plays a critical role in structuring access to important resources in the society. This situation places a great deal of pressure on schools and teachers to test, grade, and stream students. Once students are streamed, hey are then treated and taught differentially — very often they are offered a different level of the curriculum and are not accorded the same degree of respect and civility. The effects of streaming on students, teachers, morale, and discipline will be discussed in more detail in the next chapter.

The formal curriculum, however, is only one of the curricula in operation in schools. In addition to the formal curriculum, there is what is commonly referred to as the hidden or implicit curriculum. This refers to all the messages that are conveyed by the way in which the formal curriculum is presented by the teacher, and the rules (often unstated) that students have to follow if they want to succeed at the formal curriculum. The number of hours per week allocated to a subject indicates the importance that the school places on it. The methods of teaching and the way in which the teacher organizes the class for learning also convey messages to students. For example, in a lesson that is based on cooperative learning, students may learn the importance of collaborating and working together, of building on others' ideas, and of listening to gain others' perspectives. In a lesson where the teacher is the authority and the focus is on learning facts, and where students' ideas are not entertained, students may learn that knowledge is always fixed and certain, that their own ideas or experiences do not count and that there is an authority that determines what is true and correct. Students can learn much about themselves and their fellow students through the teacher/student relationship and the environment that is created in the classroom. Students can learn that they and their fellow students are worthy of respect. Or they can learn that they are undeserving of respect, or that some students, such as those in the lower streams, are undeserving of respect and understanding.

In discussing the curriculum, one can also think of the subjects and topics that are not studied in school. Because of the emphasis on knowledge and disciplines taught at the university, or on technical vocational subjects required by the job market, there is little room on the school's timetable for topics that relate to students' self-knowledge or self-development, self-empowerment or about citizenship and human relationships. The new ROSE Grade 7 to 9 curriculum, however, allows for some of this knowledge with the inclusion of Resource Management, and Home and Family Management. Nevertheless, topics such as Understanding the Self; Parents' and Children's Rights and Responsibilities; Human and Legal Rights of Citizens; You and the Law; Being a Good Consumer; Growing Up/Adolescence; and Resolving Conflicts are not usually included in the school curriculum and are presumed to be addressed during guidance and counselling sessions, or addressed in special initiatives and programmes. When they are included, as has been the case with such topics as Personal Development Programme and Family Life Education, they are often not accorded much importance by students since they are not examined. They often incorporate much of the content of disciplinary subjects such as Religious Education or Biology, and they are taught in the traditional teacher directed lecture mode – all of which reduce their impact. Yet, such issues are of vital importance to the growth and development of young people and are critical to employees' proper functioning at the workplace. The "competitive academic curriculum" leaves little room for anything else. Indeed, it has been observed that feelings and emotions are rarely discussed or addressed in classrooms (Goodlad, 1984). Many teachers are unable to address these issues adequately because they themselves have not been exposed to such discussions and their teacher education does not adequately prepare them for that role.

It is in the act of teaching that the curriculum is enacted and students are connected with the ideas, skills, and attitudes that the school has decided should be learned. Thus, the classroom transaction is important – students learn and do not learn, understand or become confused, develop a love or a disinterest in learning and ideas, based on how the curriculum is taught. In teaching the curriculum, the teacher is expected to present ideas in such a way that students engage intellectually with the subject matter, become interested in the ideas so that they want to explore and learn more. This means that the teacher has to experiment with teaching methods in order to devise strategies that will appeal to a given group of students. Although there are many approaches to teaching and learning and the particular method one chooses will be influenced to a great extent by the subject matter and the ability and age of the students, it appears learning is enhanced when students understand what is expected of them, get recognition for their work, learn quickly about errors, and receive guidance in improving their thinking or their performance (Goodlad, 1984). But in addition, there is the important question of the teacher/student relationship which is the context in which teaching and learning take place. We have seen that teachers can be engaged in different practices with different students or groups/classes of students. And students come to a particular subject or topic with different interests, abilities, and motivations to learn. "Pupils' relations with the curriculum are contained within the joint practices they construct with their teachers" (Connell et al., 1982: 104).

72

Successful teaching depends on all these elements, and in particular on the teacher's human qualities of patience, interest, and caring for students.

Another necessity for effective teaching and learning are teaching/learning materials that help teachers to convey concepts, address individual learning needs and styles, and enable students to do independent reading and research. When such materials are not available, teachers have to rely on methods such as reading the content to students, or writing what is to be learned on the chalkboard. And when students do not have the required textbooks or other learning materials, they are deprived of the opportunity to be engaged in any activity during the lesson. Such basic requirements cannot be overlooked when discussing the curriculum, teaching, and learning. But in many poor countries, these basic materials are often lacking or are insufficient. Such basic materials are often lacking in many schools in Jamaica – especially the all-age and comprehensive high schools and those attended by poor students.

The two extracts in this chapter provide examples of teaching at the secondary level. These extracts are taken from an ethnographic study of ten all-age schools in five parishes in 1988. As we saw earlier, the all-age school was and remains the most underresourced in the system. The all-age school has often been called the Cinderella of the school system – not regarded as important or equal to other schools, often ignored in planning, never an object of praise or pride. Yet roughly 40 percent of all students in Grades 7 to 9 in Jamaica are in these schools. Their students come mainly from poor rural areas – though all-age schools are also located in urban areas. At the time of the study, the official teacher/student ratio was 1:50, though classes with sixty-five or more students were not uncommon. Since then, the teacher/student ratio has been officially reduced to 1:45, although larger classes are still common in some of these schools. Noisy, overcrowded classrooms, with few available teaching materials and resources, often provide the context for teaching and learning in these schools.

The research used a combination of survey and ethnographic research methods of observation and interviewing. Observations were carried out in ten schools in five parishes over a period of four months. A total of twenty-five Grades 7 to 9 teachers and their classes were observed. These and about thirty other teachers, the ten principals, and selected students were also interviewed. We could see not only what was actually taught but how it was taught and whether it was understood by students. We were able to detect the climate and tone of classrooms, the ways teachers

73

and students interacted, and the level of active participation of students in learning.

In most of the classes observed, teachers tended to use a model of teaching that had the following characteristics: emphasis on students' completion of written assignments and the teacher's correction of these assignments; little time devoted to teacher explanations, students' questions or diagnosis of students' learning problems. The absence of textbooks contributed to this model. Without textbooks, students could not be asked to prepare for a lesson, or to interact with the content of the lesson in any meaningful way, or to do meaningful homework assignments. Nevertheless, despite the prevalence of this model of teaching which was made necessary in part because of the absence of teaching/learning materials, the researchers in this study observed four teachers who adhered to some good teaching/learning principles, and who managed to teach lessons that were considered successful. The first extract presents a lesson of one of these four teachers. In this extract, we see a teacher who is teaching with some constraints but who, nevertheless, shows respect for and encouragement of her students.

Example of a successful lesson

Subject: General Science Grade 8-2
Topic: Experiments on Elements/Compounds

1:50 Mrs B wrote up the subject Science on the chalk board; she then reminded the class,
  "I told you to look up about elements and compounds, anybody did so?"

There was no enthusiastic response, but Mrs B asked some pertinent questions to gain the responses.
She asked:
  "What are elements?"
  "How many forms are there?"

Several students were asked:
  "Jean what is your reply?"
  "Can you hear her?"
  "Let's hear what is Michael's definition?"

Finally the desired responses came out.
She then announced:
  "Today we are going to do some experiments."

Mrs B was equipped with her apparatus which she rested on the student's desk closest to the chalkboard. She then instructed the students to get two pieces of paper, one leaf from an exercise book or a folder paper cut into two. She pointed out:
  "You only need two pieces for three persons, one for sulphur and the other for iron."

She cautioned emphatically before distributing the elements:
  "Do not taste nor smell, only look."

She then moved around in the limited space distributing the chemicals stressing as she gave them:
  "I am giving you a yellow powder, sulphur; now I'm going to pass an element which is iron filing; when you file the machete that's what drops off; it looks like sand."

Mrs B then instructed:
  "Now mix the two elements; don't use your hand, remember – use something to mix them together."

At the same time, Mrs B mixed her mixture in a bottle stopper held firmly by her with a pair of forceps. As the students mixed, using pens, pencils, sticks, she asked:
  "What do you notice?"

She got the response "Don't mix," and Mrs B emphasized,
  "The iron is still seen, they don't mix; do you think you can still separate them?"

Mrs B then told them:
  "Now I am going to pass out some magnets. There are not enough for everyone; you have to share."

She did so, and encouraged the students to put the magnet in and see what happened. This activity was full of excitement, and as the filing

came up on the magnet there were comments heard in the background from the students like "Magic", "Obeah".
Mrs B then asked;
   "What have you just done?"

Paul replied:
   "We separate the sulphur and the iron filing."

Mrs B then announced:
   "OK, we are going to do another experiment."

This one she demonstrated herself, mixing the iron filing and sulphur in a beaker with water. She then passed the container with the mixture around for the students to observe and asked:
   "What do you notice?"

Some responded:
   "The sulphur is on top."
   "The sulphur is floating."

Mrs B enquired why, but she had to supply the response herself – the sulphur is lighter. She then continued, stressing some characteristics of a mixture:
   "So we can say that a mixture:
   I.   can be separated physically
   II. consists of two or more elements
   III. contains elements that can be separated."

Observer's comment: At this point the excessive noise from Grade 8 became intolerable. The students in 8-1 had just returned from their weed/shrub collecting activity and were with groups. Mrs B turned around and appealed quietly to 8-1 and finally Mrs H settled the 8-1 students, so that the 8-2 could continue.

Mrs B then asked the class:
   "What can we say about a mixture?"
A boy responded: *"A mixture consists of two things."*
Mrs B: *"Go on."*
The boy continued, *". . : that can be changed."*

Mrs B: "Good try . . . you are not wrong . . . we just would like to shape that up a little."

Andrea responded: "They are mixed together but they are not combined."

Mrs B: "I wonder if Andrea can explain that for us?"

Andrea hesitated.

Mrs B: "Anybody else wants to try?"

There were no volunteers.

Mrs B: "OK, let's think of Fitzroy's definition."

She wrote on chalkboard: "A mixture consists of two or more things . . .," then she asked a better name for things and got elements. The definition finally read:

"A mixture consists of two or more elements that can be separated physically, for example, by using a magnet or water."

She then instructed the students to write the definition, and while they were doing so, to pass up the magnets.

Mrs B soon announced,

"We have one last experiment to do. Now, we are going to do a compound. I am going to put two elements, the same amount of sulphur and iron filing in a container, then heat it."

The students had to move forward and bundle up to be able to see the experiment being performed. Mrs B used the bottle stopper, as before, held firmly with forceps. She mixed the elements, then heated the mixture over a lit candle. She asked,

"What do you notice?" as she passed the mixture around.

The students observed that there was now only one colour.

Teacher: "Can we separate it?"

She put the magnet in without success, and then noted,

"It does not attract the magnet."

She then continued to probe for more observation.

"What did you notice after the experiment?"

Response from the class:

"One colour," "Cannot be separated."

77

Teacher: *"What else? Did I just heat the sulphur, or did I just heat the iron?"*

Response: *"Consists of two elements."*

Teacher: *"What can we say then about a compound? Who can make up a definition?"*

One girl responded: *"A compound is made up of two elements that cannot be separated."*

Teacher: *"Is it just two elements that a compound can be made up of?"*

Response: *"No, Miss."*

Teacher: *"Well, do the definition again."*

Benjamin's definition: *"A compound consists of two or more elements that cannot be separated."*

This definition was written on the chalkboard for students to copy.

2:30 Mrs B then told the class that it was necessary to write out the experiments, and that this was done in a special way. She proceeded to write the first experiment, emphasizing the appropriate format and getting input from the students.

Experiment I: *To prepare a mixture from Iron and Sulphur*

Apparatus: *Magnet, water, beaker, powdered sulphur, iron filing, bottle lid*

Method: *(a) Mix iron filing and powdered sulphur in equal amounts.*

(b) Pass magnet across lid.

(c) Pour other half in beaker and add water.

Result: *(a) When iron filing and sulphur were mixed, both elements could be seen separately.*

(b) When magnet was passed across the mixture, the iron filing came up on the magnet.

(c) When water was added to the mixture, the sulphur floated on top.

2:55 Mrs B observed:

"OK, time is on us, so you will have to write up the other experiments on your own. Do that as an assignment. All I am giving you is what the experiment is."

She then wrote the experiment and emphasized the format as follows:

Experiment 2: To prepare a compound from Iron and Sulphur
Apparatus:
Method:
Result:
She furthermore hinted that they write the method and results in steps
a, b, c . . .

Observer's comments:
The observer felt this was a very good lesson from the point of view
of preparation, content, methodology and general presentation. The
students were fully engrossed; the feedback and interaction were
superb. Mrs B disclosed that she received assistance from her husband
who teaches Science at a secondary school. Even the apparatus was
given to her by him.

   We see in this extract, a teacher who shows caring and respect for her
students, a willingness to probe to address individual learning problems,
and to proceed logically in a step-by-step approach in order to ensure that
students understand at each step. At the end, we came to regard her as a
good teacher, not just a teacher who taught good lessons occasionally or
who had desirable dispositions. She placed emphasis on students' learning and understanding and tried to achieve this in a variety of ways. Like
the other good teachers observed in this study, she had to overcome the
basic problems of lack of resources, and had to find ways to make textbooks or their substitutes available. These teachers therefore differed from
the others in their interest and commitment to the task of teaching and to
students' learning, and their willingness to do additional work to make
learning meaningful and to have students engaged in learning.
   There was always a very good, easy, and respectful relationship
between Mrs B and her students. Hers was the only class where we saw
humour and easy laughter – not laughter directed at the discomfort of others, as we very often saw in other classrooms. And students always
responded with interest, attention, and involvement. As a teacher, she
was always prepared, showed evidence that she had thought through all
the steps of the lesson and the activities in which students would be
engaged. For her Science lessons, there were apparatus, materials, and
objects for use and manipulation by students. Consequently, the content

was always substantive. She obviously placed an emphasis on students' understanding, and tried to achieve this through much probing, restatement of students' ideas, discussion, and application of ideas. Students were always fully involved and interested in these lessons despite the obvious discomfort of an overcrowded and uncomfortable classroom. In her Language Arts lessons, she allowed students to use and discuss their experiences and to comment on the ideas of others. She often "worked" with the ideas of students, elaborating and refining them. And students were rarely discouraged in their halting attempts to express themselves. As she said in the Science lesson reproduced above, "Good try, you're not wrong, we just would like to shape that up a little."

The next extract is of a Language Arts lesson from the same study, and is typical of the teaching observed in most of the classrooms in this study. As described above, teaching in these schools had certain characteristics such as emphasis on teacher talk, absence of or an insufficient supply of learning materials and an absence of discussion. In addition, for most of the classes and the teachers observed, the climate was formal, often punitive and authoritarian, where teaching was mainly teacher-directed, with very little interaction between teacher and student over ideas, where the format of teaching was primarily by assignments on chalkboard followed by seatwork by students, and where much of student instructional time was spent in copying assignments and filling in blanks. In this lesson, which lasted for eighty-five minutes, the teacher began by writing sentences on the chalkboard. Each set of two sentences had homonyms, the part of speech of which students were required to identify (e.g., trade used as a noun and as a verb). The teacher began by doing some examples with the entire class.

Extract from Language Arts lesson – Example of seatwork teaching

Grade 7

9:10 a.m.
I arrive to see the door closed, a few girls outside at the window, and Miss R at her desk marking books. When I ask her if it's all right for me to be here at this time, she says yes – they'll be there doing Reading till about 9:30 a.m. I go outside to wait for a chair which is fetched by a student.

9:15 a.m.

I enter, Miss R is still correcting work. Many students are walking around, talking to each other. A few are reading. There are about forty-five students, about twenty-seven girls. I ask the boy near to me what they are doing. They're reading. His book is called *The Raid*. I ask which story is he reading. He was told by the teacher that they should "find a book and read". Other books on the desks are *The Silver Sword*. I learn from the boy that the books belong to the school and are kept in the teachers' staffroom.

The room is crowded. The 2 windows on the left have panes missing so does the one window on the right. I notice the door is now kept open after my entrance. The walls need washing or painting – so does the ceiling. There are three columns of desk/chair combinations, each combination seating three students. Miss R's class occupies two-thirds of the room which is about 40' x 30'. In the far corner is Miss T's class and the two are divided by a large chalkboard which Miss T uses.

9:20 a.m.

A box of kisko arrives and is placed on the teacher's table. After this, there is general disorder and noise as students rise and move about in both classes. Roughly one-half the class are up and about. Some children are actually eating the kisko. I later learn that they go on break around 9:15 a.m. The activity continues until 9:39 a.m. I don't hear a bell.

9:35 a.m.

Miss R rises and writes on the chalkboard <u>English Language</u> then looks at the book in hand. Now most children are in their seats and are looking at the chalkboard. She writes on the chalkboard:

In the following, tell the parts of speech of trade, feed, strike, call, mean.

(a) *Improved trade means increased prosperity and a higher standard of living.*

(b) *Our trade relations with other countries are cordial and mutually beneficial.*

(c) *The feed shop can supply our needs.*

(d) *Feed my lambs.*

(The teacher copies the above from the book.)

9:40 a.m.
She turns to the class and says:
"Remember, last time, we learned that some words can be both parts of speech. Now read these sentences and decide which part of speech it is."

All read in unison.
Teacher: "If you read the sentences you will see that they are a different part of speech. Now read the sentence again."

The boys enter from break. They read the first sentence (a).
Teacher: "Now trade, what part of speech is it?"

A few say verb, one says adverb.
Teacher: "Verb?"
Ronald: "Verb."
Teacher: "Who says it's a verb?"

Six hands go up.
Teacher: "Who says it's a noun?"

Two hands go up.
Teacher: "Ronald is right."

They go to the second sentence (b). They read.
Teacher: "What part of speech is trade?"
Student: "Verb."
Teacher: "Improved trade could never be a verb. It is not doing the work of a verb. What is a verb?"
Students: "It's a doing word."
Teacher: "Now read (b). Who can guess the part of speech?"
Two hands go up. "Verb."
Teacher: "Verb?
Student: "Adjective."
Teacher: "Yes, it's an adjective. Trade is describing relations. So it is a . . . ?"
Student: "Adverb."

82

Teacher: *"Adverb?"*
Student: *"Adjective."*
Teacher laughs.

9:45 a.m.
Teacher: *"Now let's do (c) and (d)."*

She underlines the word "feed" in both sentences.
Students read (c). She calls on Steve who says it is a noun then changes it to adverb. There are four hands. When the teacher asks what it is, a few voices say adjective then the sound rises as all agree.
"What is it describing?"
"Shop."

Teacher goes on to (d). They read the sentence. Most agree "feed" is a verb here. There are many hands.
Teacher writes: *"Make sure you have an adequate supply of feed for the poultry."*
Boy says: *"Feed is an adjective in this sentence."*
Teacher: *"Is he right? No. Why did you say it's an adjective?"*
Boy: *"It is describing adequate supply."*
Teacher (a bit surprised and impatient): *"Adequate there is the adjective and feed is the noun."*
Teacher now reads from book: *"There is a strike of workers nearly every month."*
Students call out. *"Who says it's a noun?"*
One or two students: *"It"s not a noun."*
Teacher: *"Let me read it again."*

She points to one student who says it is a verb, then another, who says it is a noun.
Teacher: *"Why do you say it's a noun?"*

A few students giggle, including the one who answered.
Teacher: *"Why? It is a noun; definitely."*

(She gives no explanation though she had asked for one).
She reads: *"They strike for higher wages, etc."*

83

Most students agree immediately that it is a verb.
Teacher reads: "We have come in answer to your call for help."

(The "h" is not pronounced.)
Most recognized "call" as a noun.
Teacher reads: "To call a spade a spade is to be nothing more or
less than frank."

Students recognize "call" as a verb. Teacher asks why but gets no
explanation (that I can hear).

9:55 a.m.
Teacher reads: "He's not a mean man. We all mean to study
hard."
(The part of speech of mean in these two sentences is correctly iden-
tified.)
Teacher says: "Now I'm going to change the words to these."

She erases trade, fee, strike etc., and writes drive, will, suit, race.

At this point I notice for the first time that the boy near me is sitting
on the broken off stump where the desk top should be. He is thus
sitting directly in front of the boy in the chair. One girl is sleeping.
The teacher leaves then returns. I notice some girls are reading
magazines while the teacher writes on the chalkboard. Both boys and
girls talk loudly among themselves – the teacher does not react.
Teacher writes: a) A few enterprising ladies are organizing a drive
to collect funds for the poor.
b) Drive evil thoughts out of your mind.
c) Where there's a will there's a way.

10:05 a.m.
The teacher finally turns around and calls to students who are talking
but in a gentle almost lifeless voice not befitting the noise and disorder that prevailed. She continues:
d) Will you take money to Mr Jones and collect the
goods for me?
e) That does not suit me, go and get another.
f) He wore his grey suit to the wedding.

The students are busy writing off sentences even though they are required only to tell the part of speech.

> g) *It does not matter who wins the race.*
>
> h) *In which race did you participate?*

10:12 a.m.

The teacher sits down and begins to work at her desk. I ask the student beside me what he's doing. He's doing the exercise on the board. He's doing English. What's the exercise? Copying down the sentences. The boy near him giggles. I ask him what is the exercise. He tells me.

10:22 a.m.

The teacher is still working at her desk.

10:25 a.m.

A few children have finished and take books to the teacher. I walk around and notice that many are just copying sentences without stating the part of speech. When I ask a few what is the task, they tell me. And one explains he copies all the sentences then goes through and writes in the answer.

Observer's comments:

There is no difference between the teaching step and the application step or seatwork in this lesson. I wonder to myself if there is a pupil culture operating against the teacher and what she tries to do. If so, what is the nature of it? Students giggle when asked to give reasons, giggle when a wrong answer is given. They seem comfortable chattering with each other or reading magazines while the teacher is at the chalkboard.

10:31 a.m.

About twelve students have lined up to have work corrected.

10:35 a.m.

The line is lengthened — about eighteen are waiting.

10:40 a.m.

A boy enters with a carton of milk and places it on teacher's desk.

I ask the teacher whether she'll spend the rest of the twenty minutes correcting work. She says yes. I leave.

We see in this extract the main features of the model of teaching described as "seatwork teaching"; that is, teaching that relies mainly on the completion of exercises, on passing on little bits of knowledge unrelated to anything meaningful or to students' experiences. In this model, the teacher spends a very short period of time in making an explanation or in assigning work. The work or task is usually written on the chalkboard. This may take about five minutes, unless the assignment is a lengthy one. The remainder of the lesson is spent with the students working individually on the assignment while the teacher sits at the teacher's table and corrects work or waits for the students to complete the assignment. If there is any teaching in the sense of helping another to learn or understand, it is by means of posing questions and awaiting responses. In almost all the examples provided by the teacher in this lesson, students obviously could not tell the part of speech and guessed the answer. They often changed their minds after guessing. The teacher accepted the guesses, without explanation or further examples and continued. After this initial segment of the lesson in which the entire class engaged in a question and answer session, the teacher spent about thirty minutes writing more sentences on the chalkboard. Students were required to complete these exercises. After ten minutes of working, students began lining up to have their work corrected. The remainder of the lesson — about forty-eight minutes — was spent in this manner, with students lining up and teacher correcting work.

This description points up the major features of the seatwork model. First, there is no introduction to the lesson. The teacher merely writes the exercise on the chalkboard. Even the directions for working — which teachers normally state verbally — are written on the chalkboard. This failure to properly introduce a lesson or to get students interested in the topic was seen in nearly all lessons observed. Second, there is little explanation or teaching, in the sense of imparting information, engendering interest, or getting another to learn. As a consequence, students' seatwork is not preceded by any learning. Third, since students have not been taught, they guess the answers, ask other students or look in other students' books, since there is no other way of determining the answer. A fourth and significant feature of this lesson is the inefficient use of time. The English Language lesson just described lasted from 9:35 a.m. to 11:00 a.m., a total of eighty-five minutes. These eighty-five minutes were used thus:

Teacher writes on chalkboard without speaking, 5 minutes
Teacher solicits answers and writes on chalkboard, 32 minutes
Students line up while teacher sits at table correcting, 48 minutes

In this lesson a great deal of time was spent with the teacher writing on the chalkboard, and students lining up to have their work corrected. The interactive segment of the lesson was not teaching – aimed at developing students' understanding. And those students who completed the exercise at 10:12 a.m. were not assigned additional work for the remaining forty-eight minutes of the period. This inefficient use of time was seen in many lessons. Teachers were observed to spend up to twenty minutes writing on the chalkboard, while students talked with each other or became restless. We saw only three teachers – at three schools – who were disposed to writing assignments on the board before the start of the lesson. This model of teaching, and in particular the writing on the chalkboard, is in part influenced by the absence of textbooks, materials and resources, and frequently students' writing materials such as exercise books and pencils. Students' lack of textbooks was a major problem in nearly all the schools in this study. On average, only 10 percent of the students had the required textbooks. The reason was that parents could not afford to purchase books. The lesson illustrates the ways in which such deficiencies can rob students of proper learning environments and learning opportunities.

What is evident from this lesson and others observed in this study is the absence of meaning or real learning or understanding on the part of students. There is also little indication of the teacher attempting to bring about such understanding and learning. An emphasis on activity without much student thinking, failure to consider students' points of view and their experiences, and a reluctance on the part of most teachers to engage in real discussion and dialogue with students made these encounters superficial and lacking in substance or interest. In addition, there is an emphasis on definitions or rule following. This may be associated with lack of explanations or efforts to get students to learn, but may be a result of the teachers' own level of understanding of subject matter. In the extract of the Language Arts lesson described above, definitions and parts of speech were the substance of the lesson. This emphasis on definitions with little reference to students' experiences or expression of ideas was noticed in most of the lessons observed. In many ways, the teaching method served as a distancing mechanism between teacher and student.

With the emphasis placed on the teacher's telling or reading bits of information and on students' being able to identify the correct answer, most teachers seemed unable or unwilling to encourage and advance learning and understanding through skilful use of children's incorrect or incomplete responses. Incorrect answers were rarely used, or analysed to further understanding, to correct misconceptions, or to develop ideas. Not only did teachers not actively solicit ideas, they quickly squashed them when students spontaneously offered them. Teachers also ignored the response or insulted or embarrassed the student when he or she made an error. This model of teaching also affects students' conception of academic work. In the lesson described above, the students conceived of the task of copying down the sentences − not even answering the questions posed. We saw many examples of students' copying work without thought or reflection.

Another consequence of this model of teaching and indeed of the absence of materials and resources to engage students' interest and provide alternative work, was the need to control students and their behaviour. If students are not engaged or are not interested or do not have the learning materials to focus their attention, or if they do not understand instructions, or do not find the task meaningful, they will show their boredom and lack of interest. Corporal punishment and verbal abuse of students were the means most frequently used by teachers to control or intimidate students. Observers noted that teachers carried the strap or cane everywhere, and the threat of corporal punishment pervaded the atmosphere of schools and classrooms. Students were beaten for a variety of reasons − for not paying attention, for not doing homework, for not having textbooks, for not understanding, for forgetting what had been learned, for making spelling errors, for arriving late. Many of these reasons were related to their academic work or academic performance.

In many cases, students did not pay attention because they were not interested in what was being taught or the material was of little interest and relevance. As a result, teachers became frustrated; the lack of satisfaction from their efforts made them resort to punishment as well as verbal abuse. Students were insulted if they were inattentive, giggled inappropriately, or laughed. But it may also be that many teachers believed that punishment was necessary to get recalcitrant students to learn. One teacher justified the use of the strap by saying, "These students won't learn anything you give them." Another teacher was heard to say while energetically beating a student who had not learned his Bible verse, "Learn them, learn them, and you rude on top of it." Corporal punishment in fact appeared to be an accepted part of school life, carried out by principals and teachers alike. One teacher said to a student who cried when beaten and complained that he had been hit in the eye: "You should not come to school if you don't want flogging." The few teachers who were prepared and/or who engaged in more interaction with their students did not have to resort to these types of punishment. And there were a few students in each class who appeared conscientious and motivated and whom the observer did not see being punished in this way.

This second extract has illustrated the ways in which the quality of teaching and learning is influenced by the context in which they take place and the materials and resources available for students' meaningful engagement with ideas. The physical context of these classrooms — overcrowded and noisy with no room for individual work or discussion — sets the stage. The absence of textbooks engendered a technology of teaching which for the most part ignored student learning. Differences in student aptitude could not be appropriately addressed. The technology was inefficient in use of time and ineffective for learning. With little or no resources (textbooks, teaching aids, materials) teachers resorted to routinized, outmoded ways of teaching. Teachers themselves seemed affected by the difficult task which they faced in attempting to teach under conditions of stress — overcrowded classrooms, noisy environments, few if any materials, and unmotivated students. Their resort to punishment may be as much a result of their dissatisfaction and frustration as it is a result of the norms of the school.

5

Streaming and Its Effects on Students

Streaming – sometimes referred to as tracking or grouping by ability – is a method of organizing teaching whereby students are categorized according to their academic ability and placed in different classes at the same grade level or in different groups within a class. Students may be separated into different classes for all subjects for the entire year. Or they may be separated for some subjects only.[1] As we have seen in chapter 4, streaming is an essential aspect of the competitive academic curriculum. In schools where this curriculum has pride of place, knowledge is derived from what is taught at the higher levels of the education system, is organized hierarchically, and usually taught in a directive, transfer mode of teaching. This knowledge is regularly tested to determine who has learned most and least. This structure places a great deal of pressure on schools and teachers to categorize students by ability so as to teach them in a uniform manner and to test them regularly. Because these examinations represent the only form of the public's evaluation of schools, the pressure to stream is even greater.

Because academic ability is of such central importance in school, streaming by ability structures the students' school experience in a very fundamental way. The student's academic ability is identified publicly and the label of high or low achiever is given to a class as well as to the students in that class. The result is that teachers and students in other classes begin to define these students according to their ability. The As are bright, the Cs are dunces, are slow to learn, and so on. As Oakes (1985) has argued, a student in a low-achieving class becomes a low-achieving person; the one in a high-achieving class becomes a high achieving person. Associated qualities are soon attributed to such students. The high achiever is also good, dependable, hard-working. The low achieving student is lazy, dull, and so on. The student's identity is therefore structured on a continuing day-to-day basis through the evaluations which are made in social interactions. In some schools and for some students, movement from one stream to a higher stream is possible. Many students, however, may spend their entire school career in a low stream.

Streaming is such a common practice in Jamaican schools that it is taken for granted by teachers and parents alike. When a student goes to school, he or she is placed in the high stream or the low stream, or, if there are three groups, in the high medium or low stream. Because of the large number of students in a class, streaming is also sometimes practiced in mixed ability classes. The policy of streaming is decided at the school level, but many teachers accept streaming as a normal way of organizing for teaching; they firmly believe that streaming makes teaching easier. Many teachers pick out or promote bright promising students. They also believe or assume that students learn better and are more comfortable when placed in a class with students of similar ability. Oakes (1985) outlines the following assumptions underlying these beliefs: that bright students' learning is likely to be held back if they are placed in mixed ability groups, that slower students will develop more positive attitudes about themselves and school if they do not have to compare themselves with brighter students, that teachers can accommodate individual differences more easily in homogenous groups, and that the basis for assigning students to ability groups is fair and just. The evidence, however, from several studies in North America and elsewhere contradicts these assumptions. Students do not benefit from homogenous groups or learn less in mixed ability groups. Placement in homogenous groups can be harmful to the self-esteem and the aspirations of those in the low streams, and the basis for allocating students to ability groups, mainly IQ tests, is not always fair and just, especially to students from different cultural and language backgrounds (e.g., Oakes, 1985; Slavin, 1993). Furthermore, it has been shown that more school resources are allocated to higher streams – the groups with more ability – with the result that those students who need more, are given less (e.g., Oakes, 1985; McNeill, 1988; Darling-Hammond, 1995).

Once students are streamed, they are treated and taught differentially; very often they are offered a different level of the curriculum and are not accorded the same degree of respect and civility. Keith (1976) has shown that in Jamaica, streaming influences the teacher's expectations and hence, the evaluations which they make of the students. And students in a low stream are not expected to do as well as those in a higher stream and their evaluations are consequently less positive. Research conducted elsewhere provides evidence for this (e.g., Oakes, 1985). A stream is not only an academic category, it is a social unit as well. Students in a particular stream associate with the other students in that class; and students in other classes begin to think of all those students as one of a kind. Students in a class are influenced by the habits, inclinations, and behaviours of the other students in that class. We saw in the study by Brown, cited earlier, that most of the boys in 3Q were prepared to cooperate with some teachers but not with others, to participate in some lessons and pay attention to some teachers and not others. And we saw how teachers came to lower their expectations for the entire class.

There is some evidence that boys and girls in the various streams have different experiences and are subject to a different type of discourse at school. In a recent study of gender and achievement at the secondary level (Evans, 1998), streaming and gender made an important difference in the school practices which students encountered. The experience of high stream girls was quite different from that of high stream boys, low stream girls, and low stream boys. The table on the following page shows that boys are more likely to be subject to negative school practices such as corporal punishment and verbal insults than girls. But in addition, the stream in which one was placed made a difference.

The table shows that there were differences by gender and stream in the number of students who reported these negative treatments and these differences were all statistically significant. Low stream boys are more subject to these negative experiences, with 29.1 percent of low stream boys reporting being insulted, compared with 17 percent of low stream girls and 8.7 percent of high stream girls. Boys and girls were more likely to dislike the way teachers treat them if they are in the low stream than if they are in any other stream.

What effect does placement in a stream have on primary students? What is school like for high and low achievers? This is the question that Yusuf-Khalil set òut to answer. She observed and spoke with students and teachers in two all-age schools and one primary school over a period of six weeks. She focused on the perspectives and the feelings which students in the A and C (high and low) streams have about school. Yusuf-Khalil's account describes some of the features of primary/all-age school classrooms such as teaching methods in which students are rarely active participants, the absence of attention to the emotional needs of students, the use of corporal punishment (beating) as a means of discipline, and an authoritarian classroom climate. But she also outlines the many ways in which classroom processes, activities, and the expectations of teachers differ by stream.

Table 1: STUDENTS' PERCEPTIONS OF SCHOOL PRACTICES BY SEX AND STREAM

	HIGH STREAM		MIXED ABILITY		LOW STREAM		x^2
	Girls	Boys	Girls	Boys	Girls	Boys	
I get beaten at school	8.7%	18.1%	8.3%	13.7%	17.0%	29.1%	High stream 20.89* Mixed ability 12.66* Low stream 17.24*
I often think of leaving school because of beatings	3.0%	6.5%	3.5%	6.6%	8.3%	11.3%	High stream 8.01 Mixed ability 19.72* Low stream 6.36
I don't like the way teachers treat me	16.7%	25.3%	20.3%	29.1%	32.0%	39.0%	High stream 11.40* Mixed ability 17.30* Low stream 4.45
I have been insulted by my teachers	3.4%	3.8%	2.5%	4.8%	8.5%	13.8%	High stream 16.22* Mixed ability 21.66* Low stream 11.86*

* Indicates a statistically significant difference

What school is like for high and low achievers

This research was undertaken to obtain information on how high and low achievers of primary school age interpret their experience of schooling. Two all-age schools and one primary school — Moonshine Primary — were included in the sample. In all, nine classes formed the sample. Intensive observation was carried out at Moonshine Primary and less intensive observation at the two all-age schools, Springs All-Age and Gates All-Age, both of which practised streaming in all classes (all names are pseudonyms). The high and low streams were observed at all schools. In addition, three mixed ability classes were observed at Moonshine Primary, where mixed ability grouping had been introduced in Grade 1 four years earlier and is now in operation in Grades 1 to 4. At Moonshine Primary, the Grade 4 classes observed were mixed ability, whereas the Grade 6 classes were grouped by ability. All pupils in Grade 6C at Moonshine have come through the school system in the lowest stream.

Ethnographic techniques used in data collection included: participant observation, focus group interviews, which brought together informants with common problems and experiences, and informal interviews and conversations which provided rich data that no other form of qualitative method could have provided. In addition, dramatization was introduced in the initial stage of the field work. This was an extremely useful strategy in getting students to express their feelings. It also provided a medium for them to express opinions which they held but could or did not wish to put in words. Field notes, tape recording of interviews, descriptions of the school environments, impressions and analytic discussions were reduced by categorizing data into relevant themes and codes. The data were then analysed using interpretive methods of analysis.

The researcher made one visit to Gates All-Age School, at which time some focus groups, individual interviews, and general observations were conducted. No further visits were made to this school because punitive practices were so obvious and students exhibited fear in speaking of their experiences.

Placement in streams

There was an obvious relationship between placement in a stream and students' socioeconomic status. Classes with low achievers comprised students of the unskilled labourers while classes with high achievers were those of professionals such as nurses, police officers and teachers. Teachers selected for these classes also assigned differential status. Only the "best" teachers are considered suitable to teach 6A, in order to prepare them for the Common Entrance Examination. Teachers who have additional duties in the school which require them to be absent from the classroom often are not given this prestigious class.

Teachers of the high achievers tended to teach such classes for a number of years and enjoy high status among colleagues and parents. Students, by virtue of the perceptions of teachers and their parents, also accorded teachers status according to the class they teach. Thus students spoke of "the C teacher" and " the A Teacher" and therefore, they were in a "dunce class" or a "bright class". It was felt that not just any teacher can teach a class. Consequently, 5A students at Moonshine Primary on promotion to 6A this academic year were at first disgruntled that the newly placed teacher who had been teaching 5B before, was not an "A teacher".

The psycho-social environment: Discipline and punishment

In the classrooms, teachers focused on academic work and paid little attention to students' feelings or emotions. And in maintaining discipline, teachers were concerned mainly with addressing those aspects of students' behaviour which interfered with the achievement of academic goals set by them. It appeared that discipline and punishment were synonymous in the eyes of teachers and students. "Beating" (corporal punishment) was the most common form of punishment followed by verbal abuse. The students, however, distinguished between "punishment" and "beating". They used the term punishment for disciplining actions other than beating. Thus, they will say: "You should be punished, not beaten."

Most classrooms took on an authoritarian atmosphere which resulted in the build-up of emotional tension. The authoritarian teacher was not peculiar to any stream but was more commonly found in classes with low achievers. In an interview with one such teacher, she revealed her traditional orientation, by quoting the maxim "Don't spare the rod and spoil the child". Observations in this class showed that students were subjected regularly to Bible verses emphasizing obedience to adult authority, as exemplified in the following justification given by Mrs Jones (a pseudonym) to a class at Moonshine Primary after a student had been beaten:

"The Bible tells us – we must not spare the rod and spoil the child. A good beating will not kill him but will keep him out of trouble."

She emphasized that because parents love their children they "correct" them. After lectures such as these, students were required to say the Bible verse – "Children obey your parents . . . " All students except one boy agreed that "Beating is for my own good." He objected only to some of the reasons for which they received beating; and the frequency and severity of the beatings. As some boys asserted:

"Sometimes, one somebody could a talk in class and de whole class get beating."
"She beat so hard, you tremble."
"When she beat yu, yu wiggle."

Beating was used quite frequently and was not accompanied by any praise in the low stream classes where low achievers predominated. Because students were beaten but rarely praised or received kind words from their teacher, corporal punishment served mainly to alienate and cause resentment among students. Students reported that they were flogged for "misbehaving" – a term that covers a range of behaviours including playing in class, giving incorrect answers, and coming to class with "sweatback" (perspiring until their clothes are wet). Students were also beaten for disruptive activities in the classroom.

There were some differences in the way teachers maintained discipline and control. Among the low streams, one inexperienced teacher allowed her students to do anything; even while she was teaching. Two of the teachers, including Mrs Jones at Moonshine Primary, maintained constant control of the class to the exclusion of students' input in decisions made at a class level. Teachers of the "A" stream, usually relied on other strategies although they sometimes used corporal punishment. One strategy which teachers were observed to use quite frequently was to compare high achievers in the "A" stream with students in the low stream and to threaten those in the high stream with a transfer to a low stream, as seen in the following reaction by a teacher of 6A:

"Class, you're noisy like 6C. If you can't behave, then I'll send you to 6C."

The teachers of the "A" stream sometimes encouraged students to monitor their own behaviour but this strategy was not observed in the "C" stream. Beating was so pervasive in the "C" stream that it was the major consideration of many students in deciding to which class they would like to be assigned:

Boy: *"I would like to go to the 6B but not with that teacher, he beat too much."*

However, most students in all streams have come to expect beating in the process of their schooling. But they had conflicting opinions about corporal punishment: Paula, a student from 6A, felt that beating was justified:

Girl (6A):   *"Sometimes it's for your own good – it's just that they beat too hard."*

Girl (6C):   *"The more yu get beating the more yu learn [she acts doubtful]."*

Boy (6C):   *"But you don't learn so much, because yu get beating – cause you fraid of it."*

Girl (6A):   *"Beating just make you afraid and you don't learn."*

Academic work

The quality of instruction causes low achieving students to experience little if any success in school. This erodes any self-esteem they may have:

Boy (6C):   *"She kill you wid writing. If dem going down the road dem put on a heap a work pon de board an yu mus dun it before she come back else she sey yu was playing."* (He received beating for playing.)

Incorrect work and other incidences that annoy the teacher were also seen to bring on the wrath of teachers, often resulting in verbal abuse.

Boy: *"She sey we not learning anything – we going to end up planting ganja . . . tun dreadlocks."*

Girl: *"She call we fool – we feel shame an a try we a try. When yu a write bout ar, yu have fi write something nice."*

Boy: *"When she nuh set no work, an wi a play she come in an would a kill off the whole a wi."*

June: *"If she smell anything she sey we nuh brush wi teeth or wash wi socks."*

Researcher: *"Do you think she might be saying these thing to make you better?"*

June: *"No, miss! She mek we worse – mek yu ashame how she tell wi – she talk loud an in patois."*

In addition, some students also feel victimized and experience a loss of self-esteem because of where they live.

Boy: *"Teacher ask mi where mi live den she say she don't like the Pen children."* (He lives at Thompson Pen.)

When such things happen, students receive very little support because parents seldom listen to their complaints.

Researcher: *"What do your parents say about the beating?"*

Pupils: *"Some kill yu with lick too."*
"Some don't say anything."
"Dem sey dem use to get more than dat!"

Teachers reported that unlike the parents of the high achieving students who will sometimes check on the progress of their children, the parents of low achievers rarely do so.

Teacher: *"Parents don't come and check on students – only if yu knock them. But dem can't come to mi yu nuh! Mi dey ya too long."*

Streaming and students' self-evaluation

Children's self-definitions are largely based on the processing and interpreting of cues and signals given by others and on the individual's self-assessment in the light of their daily experiences with parents and peer group. In this environment, students perceived that they were treated differently and that this differential treatment was a consequence of their academic ability. They used this information for social comparison. Although some schools try to disguise the fact that the different classes are streamed by ability, students were usually aware of the distinctions. Some teachers by their word and deed made it clear to students. They were not averse to discussing individual students or groups of students in their presence or within hearing distance.

Boy in 6C: *"6A children dem in brighter class."*
Researcher: *"How do you know?"*
Girl: *"Teacher dem talk an wi hear. Teacher dem sey we inna dunce class."*

Students evaluated themselves on the basis of their stream placement. In response to the request – "Tell me about the class you're in and what you think about it" – pupils in the "A" stream spontaneously told me that "we're in the brightest class" or "we're in the scholarship class". All high achievers spoke positively about themselves. They expressed their feelings of pride at being in the "brightest class in the grade" and believed they were there because they are "intelligent". Some students remarked:

"I would cry if I was sent to 6C – I would feel shame."
"I wouldn't want to go to school."

Students in the low streams, however, regularly received negative evaluations from their teachers.

Boy: *"Dem sey wi don't know 'A' from bull foot."*
Researcher: *"How does that make you feel?"*
Group: *"We feel bad."*
Students: *"She tell wi sey wi a cruff."*
   "As dem look pan yu so dem sey you a cruff."
   "She sey wi no learning anything we guan end up planting ganja; bun coal, tun dreadlocks!"
   "When she talk the children laugh at yu and mek you feel shame."
   "See unu, that's why you don't learn, because you won't listen."

Parents' reaction to their children's placement in the "C" stream was often just as damaging to their self-esteem.

Girl: *"Some curse yu because yu not in 6A."*
Boy: *"Wi parents' don't feel good bout the class wi in."*
Girl: *"Dem say a dunce – wi feel bad."*

99

Low stream students also received negative evaluations from the students in the upper streams. For example, the students in 6A made this assessment of those in 6C:

"The 6C children are noisy."

"They behave badly; fight in front of the teacher and curse bad words."

The low stream students reported these evaluations from students in the upper stream:

They want to describe you – "Look how that girl clothes dirty and smell bad – yu arm smell."

"Sey we have no home training and respect and we a di worse class."

Such treatment made the low stream students retaliate aggressively:

Girl: *"Wi don't like dem – dem cut dem eye at wi – we cut back we eye."*

Boy: *"We boase pon dem back – we beat them up in cricket."*

The degree of animosity between the two streams varies from school to school but there is no denying that the "systems of status" produce devastating consequences for students in the low stream. The "C" stream seemed quite aware of the unacceptable behaviours mentioned by the students in the "A" stream. In fact, some began to redefine themselves on the basis of these perceptions. They did not contradict much of what students in the "A" stream said of them. Instead they expressed a wish to be in the "A" stream. They remarked that if they were promoted to "A" stream they would do their work and tidy themselves. They seemed to be of the opinion that, simply being in 6A would make them bright. Others – all boys – refused to admit openly that they wanted to be in the "A" stream or that they thought those students "better" than they. They appeared to use anger as a mechanism to defend the self.

Boy: *"Let 6A go wey, dem nuh better than we."*

Boy: *"They are not better than us, some of them can't do the work we do, I ask them something aready, and them couldn't answer."*

Some students believe that placement in a stream sends them messages about what behaviour is expected of them. The following sentiments were expressed by girls in 6A.

6A Girls: *"I think it depend on the class. In 6A, you know you must set example."*

"They know they are slow and it does not matter."

"I was in 3C – I played a lot – I didn't try, but I don't know why. When I went in 5C, I worked hard to come into a better class – since I come in 6A I play a lot."

The comment of this last student suggests that placement in a low stream can make some students develop a sense of inadequacy. They come to believe that they are unable to learn. One 6C boy reflected the feelings of many as he disclosed his secret feelings:

"I wish I could be bright so none a dem can't sey them better than us."

Streaming and school activities

A common perception held by low achievers is that high achievers are better treated by the principal and teachers in the school. Low achievers believe that 6A students are not treated like 6C because "the teacher is nicer" and "she nice to dem because dem can do their work". Low achievers made these assessments based not only on what they heard but also on the activities they were asked to do around the school and the activities from which they were excluded. As one boy in 6C observed:

"The dirty work lef for 6C, 6A don't have to do it."

It was observed that administrators usually go to the "C" stream to find students to do errands such as washing of stairs, tidying the library, carrying chairs. Such activities often extend into their class time. However, there were occasions when these same students used these activities as an opportunity to "escape" from the classroom.

The low achievers were often denied opportunities to engage in activities that could bring pride to the individual and the school. Some students in 6C remarked thus:

"They don't say anything to our class about Festival Art."

The high achievers had the advantage of representing their school in competitions. Although it is often assumed that it is the low achievers who excel in the physical and aesthetic areas, this was not the case in this study. In fact, there was a tendency for the same students to be included in a number of different activities – Art, Cricket, Festival competition, 4-H club, and the like. These students were from the "A" stream or the high achievers in the mixed-ability classes. One teacher, who was interviewed, agreed that low achievers could be included in competitions such as Art but admitted that they are excluded because, "It takes a longer time to work with slow learners and most times we don't have the time."

Teachers of mixed-ability classes did not differ significantly in their practices from teachers in streamed classes. They maintained stable, homogeneous groups in their classes, a practice which produced similar patterns of teaching as those seen in the classes which were streamed. The low achievers in these mixed-ability classes were also isolated and treated differently in the class. Although the high achieving and average students in the mixed-ability class spoke with the low achieving pupils, they would not sit in the group with low achievers, for they did not want to be associated with the low-achieving group. Students in these classes also argued that the low achievers are those "giving the most trouble" and used that to justify the fact that low-achieving students receive more physical and verbal abuse. Thus, low-achieving students, whether in mixed-ability or streamed classes, had very different experiences from the higher achieving students. Not only did teachers have lower expectations for their performance, they were stigmatized by teacher and students alike.

In this study, students in the low streams were more often beaten and verbally abused by teachers than those in the middle or high streams; they suffered differential treatment in many other ways such as the requirement to do school chores. The Creole was often used to show the teacher's contempt for a particular individual. Teachers created and further reinforced difference by the frequent comparisons between the high and low streams, and by negative evaluations of low streamers in the presence of high streamers. Such practices were done in order to coerce high streamers to act in accordance with classroom rules or to make them do their work. Distinctions were made between students with respect to their personal characteristics, their social background, their place of residence – all of which have little to do with the main purpose of school. When streaming occurred within a class, the low streamers formed a separate group often sitting at the back of the class. In most cases, the majority of this group were boys. Students thus had many opportunities to recognize the differences in status between students in the high stream and those in the low stream. Those who were in the higher streams adopted the attitude of teachers in interacting with students from the low streams. Those in the low streams began to define themselves according to this system of status. This led to unhealthy self-evaluations on the part of students. But personal animosity also developed between the two groups of students. One group suffered pain and humiliation by the words or actions of another group. The words of the low achievers reflected their deep resentment.

The extract also showed that some teachers tried to have low achieving students accept their situation. Students were asked to consent to the fact that corporal punishment (beating) is good for them; the words of the Holy Bible are sometimes invoked to justify such assertions. In some cases, the teachers succeeded in their indoctrination. Some students agreed that such beating was good for them although they objected to the frequency and severity of it. But many others resisted in subtle ways and learned to cope with the adversity of the classroom by adopting strategies of flattery and subservience while secretly resenting teachers, their power and control. These feelings of resentment and anger smouldered but rarely were given expression except in aggressive behaviour toward other students.

Yusuf-Khalil did not set out to determine the academic effects of streaming practices on students. But we know that placement in a low stream has a negative effect on academic performance, students' sense of self and their self-esteem. Streaming limits access to knowledge and quality teaching for those students in the low streams. While students come to school with different experiences, and abilities, the school appears to reinforce those differences, to create and support other differences and eventually to widen differences in students' academic performance. In many cases, the curriculum – what is taught in the low stream – is quite different from what is taught in the high stream (Oakes, 1985; Page, 1989). Streaming affects their attitude to school and their aspirations for the future. Students' identity is structured in very fundamental ways by placement in streams. The stigma which in this study resulted from streaming has been shown elsewhere to be associated with lowered academic achievement (e.g., deVos, 1992). This study also shows that schools can create alienation, animosity, resentment, and feelings of superiority and inferiority among students from different social groups.

Since this was a case study of nine classes, the study may not reflect the experiences of low stream students in all schools. But it illustrates the ways in which streaming interacts with social class. In chapter 7, we shall examine the ways in which streaming intersects with gender as well. Students experience schooling as a member of a class and gender; the reality of their schooling is as a working-class, low stream girl, or as a working-class high stream boy. And these experiences are different from those of the middle-class low stream boy or a middle-class high stream girl. The important features of the low stream working-class experience are: humiliation and shame as a result of being placed in a low stream, social and academic comparison with students of other streams, animosity and put-downs by students in other streams. Since working-class parents are not socially positioned to engage with the school and with teachers regarding the treatment of their children in school, these students receive very little support and understanding from parents. A cultural studies and postcolonial perspective would highlight the class differences in the treatment that these students receive in school, the legacy of this treatment toward children of the poor, and the contradictions evident on the part of the teachers who are themselves mainly from the peasant and working class, the contradictions evident in their misuse of the Creole which is also their language. This perspective would also point to the students' lack of voice and their ineffective attempts at resistance. They had no one to whom to voice their anger and sense of injustice (except in this case, to a researcher) and their only recourse was aggressiveness to those who caused them pain.

Streaming has benefits for the teacher, but we have to compare these benefits with its human and social cost. Although teachers must take initial ability into account in planning and organizing for teaching and learning, there are alternative ways of doing this which do not include streaming. For those committed to equality of educational opportunity, the issue of streaming is an important one and presents a problem which has to be solved. The critical educational question which faces us is what materials, resources, and approaches are needed in our schools to enable all students to have equal access to knowledge and learning experiences which allow all students or nearly all to have more or less equal outcomes. The pervasiveness of streaming in our nation's schools may be as much as a result of the limited resources and the high teacher/pupil ratio existing in these schools as the fact that streaming is a taken for granted feature of schools — a part of a tradition. This study also shows that a change of attitude on the part of teachers toward these students — many of whom are poor and male — is long overdue.

6

Language in the Classroom

Like many other postcolonial societies where speakers of different languages have come in contact, Jamaica has a Creole language derived from the languages of the colonizer and the colonized and the language of the former colonizers is more extensively accepted. Because the standard language, in this case Standard Jamaican English (SJE), is closely associated with the dominant social and economic classes, it has more prestige and status and its use is mandatory for certain social and public situations. The Creole language, in contrast, is low in status and prestige, derived as it is from oppressed slave societies and the poor marginalized groups in the society. In such bilingual speech communities, the extent to which a speaker will become bilingual will depend on the pattern of social stratification in the society, the position of a particular speaker within this pattern, and the nature and extent of the interaction between the social classes (Craig, 1978: 102–3). In Jamaica, SJE has historically been the language of a tiny minority of the upper and middle classes who had acquired this speech ability by virtue of the language of their parents or through education. Creole is the language of the vast majority of the population.

Historically, Creole has been seen as a debased form of SJE, and the Creole speaker is regarded by speakers of SJE as uneducated and uncouth. In the past, the Creole speaker has even made these self-evaluations. This situation has changed in recent years. Many Jamaicans now identify strongly with the Creole and regard its use as an expression of their sense of self or their identity; they take pride in Creole as a symbol of their Africanness. The once marginalized language is now beginning to be used more frequently in everyday discourse, in newscasts and radio talk shows, and in novels. Those who are competent in SJE often choose to speak Creole for a variety of reasons, for example, to communicate emotions and ideas more effectively, and to establish community. As a result, today, there is less stigma attached to the use of Creole. Nevertheless, despite these changes, language or the use of SJE and Creole remains very contested, with some groups in the society still decrying the use of Creole in certain social situations and referring to the language in pathological terms.

In speaking of Creole and SJE one is referring to two extremes. It is rare in any speech situation that one will hear a pure form of one or the other. In Jamaica, Creole and SJE represent points on a continuum with some combination of the two in between. That is, a speaker may combine elements of Creole with elements of SJE. This combination is referred to as a mesolect, with the different forms of each language shading off gradually along this continuum. The mesolect resembles SJE in many respects and one may even think that there are few differences between them (Craig, 1981). Shields (1989) has argued that SJE has taken on Creole features (cited in Bryan, 1998: 22).

Historically English has played a very important role in the institutions of the society – especially in the educational system. From the early days following the establishment of the elementary education system in Jamaica to the present, English was seen as the native tongue of Jamaica and the privileged. The acquisition of English and later SJE was seen as an important goal of education, and the difficulties that children had in speaking English were not acknowledged by the inspectors of the nineteenth and early twentieth centuries (Bryan, 1998: 79). There was, as a consequence, much emphasis on the teaching of English grammar. Since there was such respect for English, the Creole had no place in schools. This attitude to Creole and to SJE remained unchanged up to recently.

In recent times, there has been a change in thinking about what constitutes a language, and consequently about Creole and its place in schools. In the 1980s, the English teachers recognized the validity of the use of Creole in the Jamaican classroom. They advocated that teachers should accept and validate the child's first language or at least not to denigrate the language children bring to school. Today, many teachers accept that position. Many would also be willing to use the Creole to explain a concept where this is necessary. There is less consensus on the use of Creole as a language of instruction, though there are few individuals outside the primary and secondary school system who advocate such an approach. A reluctance to use Creole as the language of instruction stems from a variety of concerns. As Bryan (1998: 39) has explained, part of the problem might be orthography or the system of spelling for the language, as well as the lack of a well-developed connection to the traditional disciplines, research and scientific cultivation. But there is still some conflicting and contradictory attitudes on the part of teachers to the use of Creole in schools. Today, as we have seen in the extract from research by Yusuf Khalil (1993), teachers sometimes use Creole to denigrate students. When some teachers wish to insult a student, they may use the Creole – an act that signals their lack of respect for the Creole, for the child's native language as well as for the child.

Regarding the teaching of SJE, Craig (1981: 2) has argued that it is because there is a language continuum from Creole to SJE that there is a misperception that the everyday speech of West Indians is not much different from the local standard English, and that teaching and learning of SJE is relatively straightforward. This misperception obscures the major structural differences between Creole and SJE which have important implications for the teaching and learning of SJE by Creole speakers. Many teachers of English face this very challenge on a daily basis. Because of these structural differences, the Creole-speaking student experiences major problems in speaking and writing SJE. There is also still an emphasis on grammar, prescriptions about correctness of English, and an emphasis on drill and repetition; an exam orientation encourages streaming. Nevertheless, students find it difficult to communicate in the written and oral form of SJE. Examination results reveal that most students, after five years of secondary schooling, have not mastered the fundamentals of English comprehension and expression. Only 41.2 percent of those who sat English Language in the CXC examination in 1998–99 passed at Grades 1, 2 and 3 at the General Proficiency Level (CXC Statistics, 1999). These results are not very different from those obtained in 1988. Performance in the SSC is even worse. These low levels of achievement have been the norm for a number of years and have led to concerns among educators about teaching methods and their effectiveness.

There have also been concerns about the schools' preparation of students for the workplace. Only a minority of secondary graduates are able

107

to demonstrate competence in written and spoken English. During the 1980s as today, employers complained that graduates of the schools are ill-equipped to communicate in English and many organizations have been compelled to offer instruction in communication or writing skills as part of their basic in-house training. This situation and the ongoing debate about Creole, its value and place in education and the society led the president of the Rotary Club in 1989 to decide to sponsor an experimental project aimed at improving the teaching of English. The project was called "Operation English". I acted as a consultant to the project and was responsible for the documentation and evaluation. The extract below is taken from an evaluation of the project that I conducted. It illustrates a methodology in which Creole – the students' language – was respected and validated, teaching/learning materials encouraged student expression, students' language and experience were respected and students were encouraged to use SJE in meaningful contexts. The results of the study show that students learn to speak and write SJE when such teaching methods are used. In this study, most Creole-speaking students improved their ability to speak and write SJE, though the gains within the short time span were modest and sometimes inconsistent. Moreover, some students developed a more positive attitude toward SJE; their ability to speak SJE significantly enhanced their self-esteem. The results however, indicate that changes in language use from Creole to SJE must be seen in the long term.

Creole and Standard Jamaican English in the secondary classroom

Introduction and background

The study was undertaken to examine the implementation and progress of an innovation – a modified English curriculum – and to evaluate its achievement. The focus of the project was on the development, implementation, evaluation, and promotion of teaching learning strategies for the teaching of English. The project was planned for three years. This report documents what was achieved during the first year in Grade 7. It also documents the activities and discussions engaged in and the reactions of students and teachers to the new teaching/learning activities.

Research design and the setting

All six groups of Grade 7 students at the school participated in the programme. These students formed the experimental group. One group of Grade 7 students at another high school in the Corporate Area functioned as a control group for the purpose of comparing gains in achievement. Students from the two schools came from a similar socioeconomic background. The control group did not participate in the programme. All six Grade 7 English teachers were observed over the period of the academic year – two each term – and all were interviewed at regular intervals throughout the year. The project coordinator was also interviewed at regular intervals. The techniques used to obtain information on the effectiveness of the teaching/learning materials and activities included observation, interviewing, informal conversations, journal keeping, and examination of site documents such as curriculum and lesson outlines. Selected students were interviewed informally about four times throughout the year.

Journal keeping was another important data-gathering device. Both teachers and students kept journals. Teachers were asked to keep track of their thoughts on aspects of the methods and activities in order to get additional evidence on their effectiveness, to gain an insight into teachers' beliefs, and to obtain further information related to the teaching of English. Students were asked to keep journals to encourage them to express their ideas and experiences in writing and thus to develop in them a disposition to write. The students' journals were also intended to provide information on their reactions to and assessments of the activities. As the researcher, I attended planning sessions, project staff meetings and other activities in order to get first-hand information on the progress of the project and this was in addition to the data-gathering devices described above.

A writing diagnostic test (pre-test) was administered to all Grade 7 students in the experimental group at the high school and the control group of forty Grade 7 students in September 1989. The same test was again administered to these students in June of 1990. Reading and comprehension tests were also administered during the second term when it was discovered that there was a wide range of reading ability within a class.

Data analysis

Written responses to the pre- and post-test were analysed by conducting error analyses. Each written work was read and the types of errors made were noted. The responses of forty students were examined in greater detail. In these, the number of instances of an error or omission was calculated and compared with the number of occasions when the particular form or structure was required in the passage. This method of analysis allowed for a better understanding of the progress made by the student when the pre- and post-tests were compared. Comparisons between the performance on the pre-test and the post-test was done by the error analysis of these forty pieces of writing. Simple aggregates were made of the differences between the number of errors made in the responses of these two tests. In addition, teachers' assessment of qualitative differences between the two tests done by all 240 students (e.g., in the richness of ideas, the length of the written work) was also considered. Journals were also examined for errors and improvements in expression over time. All other documentary data, for example, field notes of observation and interviews, were analysed qualitatively.

Addressing characteristics and needs

We began by examining the existing Language Arts programme at the high school and the needs of students which have to be addressed. Teachers outlined the following problems:

- Students had major problems with structure and grammar.
- Students were lacking in self-confidence in general, as well as in expressing themselves verbally. Thus there was a need for students to express themselves orally.
- Students also had serious difficulties in comprehending written material. This was evident in all curricular subjects.
- Students were ill at ease with the English language. They lacked confidence and were hesitant when speaking. Many were convinced that they must use big words to demonstrate their competence.
- Most students had difficulty with spelling. One reason for this is that few students read other than the assigned textbooks.
- Students coming from the primary school were not accustomed to writing or expressing themselves orally. Thus, the programme had to provide an orientation to these activities.

Curriculum and teaching learning principles

These student characteristics influenced the design of the teaching/learning activities to be described later. In addition, all teachers at the high school were asked to do the following:

- Carry out reading in the content (subject) areas. Every teacher is a teacher of English and should use opportunities to develop reading skills (e.g., making inferences, gathering information).
- Be aware of the language programme so that they reinforce it in their own teaching.
- Be realistic in their expectations for Grade 7 students. They would not reach perfection by the end of Grade 7.
- Pay attention to handwriting.
- Always create an atmosphere in the classroom for learning.

The teachers and the programme coordinator articulated some basic principles such as integration within Language Arts as well as across subjects. Reading would be emphasized; at the same time, teachers were expected to create the proper environment and provide incentives for students to read. It was necessary to cater to different ability levels, emphasize both oral and written English, and develop a variety of activities that would provide experience and practice in speaking and writing and encourage student expression. These activities would be such that they build student confidence and self-esteem. In addition, students would learn in groups or teams. Structure would not to be taught as a topic in isolation (as it is frequently taught in many Jamaican schools), but included as part of activities where students used language in functional ways.

Teachers were encouraged to place value on both Creole and Standard English, recognizing that Creole is the students' language, the medium in which they normally and with ease express their ideas. Correcting students' language therefore should be done in a way that honoured this principle. One recommended approach was to remove the Creole phrase from the sentence in which it was used and discuss its Standard English equivalent. In this way the student eventually becomes bilingual and at the same time maintains a healthy respect for Creole.

Activities

The following were agreed upon:

- Activities should encourage/allow students to verbalize more. This could be done in their own register initially, with efforts increasingly made for them to speak in Standard English. Thus, students were required to carry out activities in groups without the help of a teacher. This arrangement would facilitate oral expression and the willingness and ease to do so. The first few lessons would therefore emphasize discussions and self-expression without regard to curricular content.

- Students should do more functional writing. Many students are shy and indisposed to discuss their experiences which they often consider deficient. Hence teachers would plan tasks which use or build on their experiences. This would build confidence and help them to value their own experience.

The teaching/learning activities which formed the programme for the first term comprised eight units (referred to as activities) as under:

- Introductory games – these activities were designed to allow students to talk about themselves and get acquainted with each other
- Experiences with the Common Entrance
- Exploring one's feelings
- The self in relation to others
- Use of leisure
- Fear
- Male/female role – What do you think?
- You and your language

These activities were intended to give students maximum opportunity to express themselves orally. This, it was hoped, would get them accustomed to speaking in public, and would develop some confidence in self-expression. Some of the teaching/learning methods used included interviewing, self-reports, group discussion, and evaluation of presentations. In all cases, personal experiences provided the focus. Journal writing was an important activity during the year. All students were required to keep journals in which they recorded personal thoughts and reactions to class activities. The rationale for journal writing was twofold: it was a research tool which allowed us to gain insights into students' appreciation of and reaction to the teaching/learning activities and to note any changes in attitudes toward the use of Standard English. It also provided an excellent means for students to express themselves in writing and, it was hoped, to improve their writing ability. Teachers were exhorted to encourage students to write and to respect students' desire to keep the contents of the journal private. If students asked the teachers to read their journals, teachers were to refrain initially from correcting students' self-expression.

The curriculum or subject matter was organized around the following themes:
- The Senses and Communication
- You and Your Language
- Organizing and Classifying Things

The six teachers were provided with an orientation to the project and the research as well as training in skills associated with the research such as journal writing. Throughout the year, they also attended regular workshops on teaching skills and methods. There were also consultations between individual teachers and the Project Coordinator on specific concerns or problems related to teaching.

Students and their attitudes to language

Jamaican Creole was the language of the overwhelming majority of the students, their home and community. It was their normal medium of expression, and the language in which they expressed themselves most comfortably. Grade 7 students, however, have spent at least six years in a primary or all-age school where they have studied English grammar, read books written in English and heard adults speak SJE. They live in a society where both SJE and Jamaican Creole are used in written and verbal communication. During English lessons they normally communicated with one another in Jamaican Creole, though they changed register somewhat when they addressed the teacher. They therefore understand and have developed certain attitudes toward SJE and Jamaican Creole.

All students who were interviewed agreed that it is necessary for one to know how to speak SJE. The reasons given were primarily utilitarian. Proficiency in spoken English would gain the respect of others and would greatly facilitate the obtaining of a job. It is needed for career advancement. Furthermore this proficiency makes one feel proud, "big", mature, impressive. Proficiency in SJE is necessary if one wants to travel or widen one's horizons. However, the majority of students interviewed did not think that SJE had to be spoken at all times. The Creole was reserved and seemed appropriate for conversations among friends and family.

Despite this acknowledgment, some students — nearly all of them boys — come to high school thinking it is "funny", almost embarrassing to speak SJE in public. This attitude existed in varying degrees in all classes but was particularly evident in one of the six classes. This attitude to SJE initially hampered efforts to get students to express themselves and to develop confidence in speaking SJE. However, as will be shown later, there was during the year a major change in students' willingness to speak SJE and to accept corrections in their speech.

Although students admitted that it was important to speak SJE, they felt inhibited when it came to speaking the language. Students reported in their diaries that they felt self-conscious, worried that they would make mistakes, and acutely aware of their unfamiliarity with SJE. These perceptions had different effects on different students during the first term. Some were halting and hesitant in speech; some, according to the teachers, used "big words" to compensate for their perceived inadequacy. Others refused to participate, at least initially. At the same time, students reported that they felt important and proud when they believed that they spoke SJE correctly.

Students' initial competence in Creole and SJE

The students, coming from a Creole-dominated environment communicate fluently and spontaneously among themselves in Jamaican Creole. In nearly all cases this was done at the extreme end of the language continuum. When they tried to move along the continuum in an effort to speak SJE, they rarely accomplished this without errors. These errors were evident in speaking, reading, and writing. Before these errors are described some differences between SJE and Jamaican Creole will be outlined.

The major differences between Jamaican Creole and SJE lie not in the vocabulary or the pronunciation, though these are significant, but in grammar and syntax. Jamaican Creole uses constructions which are derived from the Niger-Congo languages of Africa (Cassidy, 1961). It also modifies some grammatical rules of SJE. These differences mean that words are often put together differently in Jamaican Creole and SJE to express the same idea. Grammatical rules which the English speaker anticipates are not used in Jamaican Creole. Though there are many examples of these grammatical and syntactical differences (see Cassidy, 1961 for a full discussion) three will be described briefly because they recurred so frequently in students' speech and writing. They are the expression of the past tense, inflection in the present tense, and the declension of pronouns.

Jamaican Creole expresses time (tense) and aspect, that is, the condition or quality of the action/activity in a manner different from SJE. Whereas SJE relies on the inflection of the verb to express the past tense (e.g., by adding "ed"), Jamaican Creole uses other means of expressing "pastness". Three methods cited in Pollard (1987) are past auxiliaries such as "ben" or "bin", adverbial phrases of time, and reliance on the context of the sentence. A listener to Jamaican Creole who is ignorant of these syntactical conventions may conclude that Jamaican Creole ignores the rules of SJE and is, therefore, a lower form of English or is broken "bad" English. Students rarely used the inflected form of the verb to express past time. These students knew the past form and could recite it when asked by the teacher. They had learned such forms in their structure classes in primary school. Yet they avoided its use in their speech.

The lack of inflection in Jamaican Creole is also seen in the present tense. Whereas SJE will inflect the verb to express plurality in some cases, Jamaican Creole uses the same form of the verb (usually the infinitive without to) for both singular and plural. The Jamaican Creole speaker therefore almost always uses this form (which in SJE is considered the plural form) with singular subjects. It is very common to hear Jamaicans say "Mary have" or "he have". While the Jamaican Creole speaker is following a different syntactical rule, it is easy for the Standard Jamaican speaker to conclude that the speaker violates the SJE rule of concord.

In SJE pronouns have different forms for first person singular and plural (I, we), different forms for the subjective and objective cases (e.g., I/me, we/us) and different forms for gender (e.g., her, him). Jamaican Creole, however, unlike SJE (but like other Indo-European languages such as French and Spanish) has a singular and plural form for the English you, i.e., you (singular) and unnu (plural). The plural

115

pronoun "dem" is used in Jamaican Creole to pluralize nouns – a different approach from that found in SJE which inflects the noun usually by adding an "s".

These syntactical rules are always used in Jamaican Creole spoken at the extreme end of the continuum. When the student tries to move along the continuum, modifications are made to these rules, though the Creole interference is still evident. For example, in class assignments students rarely used the word "dem" to pluralize. Rarely did they use the form "me" where the SJE "I" would have been appropriate. But other Creole structures were frequently detected in their speech. At the same time, some students in their effort to speak SJE (i.e., move along the continuum) tried to adopt SJE rules with unusual results. The following are examples taken from the lessons observed during the first term:

He don't like. (The present form of the verb not inflected.)

Some doesn't have any meaning. (Attempt to adopt inflection.)

'Im teef you see, miss. Dem shoot him de oder day and dey say him should dead. (Single form "dem" used as subject, noun [teef] used as an adjective, an adjective [dead] used as a verb.)

Unnu listen please. (Plural form of you.)

He did not born in Kingston. (Wrong auxiliary.)

Although it has been asserted that syntax and grammar represent the most distinctive differences between Jamaican Creole and SJE, vocabulary and pronunciation are nonetheless significant. Some examples of the latter are evident in the examples shown above ("teef" for thief, "oder" for other). Other examples which occurred frequently were the dropping of "hs" after t (e.g., I "t'ink", "t'ank" you), or at the beginning of a word "obbies" for hobbies, "er" for her.

The above are typical errors which were detected when students attempted to speak SJE. However, there were differences among students in the number of errors made. Put another way, some students were able to move along the speech continuum with more ease than others. However, the number of students who initially functioned in the main near the SJE end of the continuum was very small, perhaps less than 10 percent.

Students' initial writing ability

Another major area of language which the project focused on was writing. This was so, not only because writing is an important and essential part of the school curriculum, but also because the act of writing allows the student to express thoughts and ideas. It is a skill necessary in all school subjects. The diagnostic writing test administered during the first weeks of the project provided information on students' initial ability. The test comprised three sections, each section testing the ability to write in the past tense, the future or future conditional and the present tense respectively.

The results of the test revealed that many of the problems of Creole interference evident in students' speech became very pronounced in their writing. They often applied Jamaican Creole syntactical rules or used Creole expressions in a SJE sentence (see pages 114–16 for a discussion of some of these rules). The main problems can be summarized as follows:

- Absence of tense markers or inflection to indicate past time
- Lack of inflection of the verb when used in the present tense
- Lack of inflection of the verb for the present participle
- Use of one form of the pronoun for all cases and as an adjective
- Creole method of pluralization
- Inadequate adoption of SJE rules
- Inconsistent use of tense markers
- Use of Creole words and phrases
- Absence of the auxiliary "be" to express continuous action
- Use of an adjective to express action

Examples of these are given below:

1. Absence of tense markers or inflection to indicate past tense

We have seen that Jamaican Creole does not use inflectional suffixes to mark the tense. Thus, the Jamaican Creole speaker/writer uses what appears to be the present tense (i.e., the infinitive without "to"). This was a very common error in students' answers to Section I of the diagnostic test. Only about 5 percent of the students did not demonstrate this weakness. A sentence such as the following was quite typical:

> "I was so anxious to reach my destination, and when we travel and travel we jump and make a lot of noise in the mini-bus."

This absence of inflection was evident in past participial adjectives (e.g., I was thrill) and in the past participle of the preterite (e.g., you have already add the water).

Many students (about 30 percent) did not have a problem with the past tense of irregular verbs (which are not inflected at the end but changed entirely). Thus, sentences such as the following were written:

"The next day when the other children saw me they call me Jesus. Sometimes I got angry and curse them."

However, students were often ignorant of the correct form of the irregular verb, and used such words as "slided", "falled", "cutted", "dropt".

Some of the few students who attempted compound sentences with a subordinate temporal clause had difficulty. In the following example, the student is speaking of a "past" time in the main clause (single past) and an anterior past time (pluperfect) in the subordinate clause.

"After we done looking at the animals we go over to the roaler [sic] coaster."

The absence of inflection was also evident when students expressed the passive voice. It is seen in the following:

"The building needed to be paint."
"Every minute somebody get rob."
"The last time some thieves rob the shop, one of them got a chop off hand and chop off finger."

2. Lack of inflection of the verb when used in the present tense

This represents another form of the problem discussed above. Jamaican Creole does not adopt inflection. Since inflection only applies to the third person singular in SJE, this was the problem area. Teachers often referred to this as lack of concord. But it can be regarded as the inappropriate application of a Jamaican Creole rule. Some examples were:

"The landlord don't want to fix it."
"The government have to deal with that."

3. Lack of inflection – present participle

Jamaican Creole, unlike SJE, does not inflect the verb after adverbs or certain verb phrases. The following are examples:
   "Instead of the boys try and do something."
   "Rob them by go into their shop."
   "To have more police patrol in the community."

4. Use of one form of the pronoun for all cases and as an adjective

The pronouns "me" and "him" were often used for the subject. There were fewer instances of "me" being used in the objective case. The following are examples:
   "One day, me, my brother and my mother were going to Mandeville."
   "Me and my friend was on the bus."
   "Give we a contribution."
   "Wash off they skin."

5. Creole method of pluralization

Cassidy (1961) states that some of the African languages from which Jamaican Creole is derived do not inflect for plurality. Those that do, do so at the beginning rather than at the end of the word. Jamaican Creole, as a result, has dispensed with pluralization by inflection. In Jamaican Creole, therefore, the noun has only one form, usually the singular, though sometimes the plural form is used (e.g., teeth, lice). Plurality, however, can be expressed in Jamaican Creole by the use of the word "dem". These Jamaican Creole rules were evident in students' written work. The following are examples:
   "The boy dem in de bus was making up plenty nize [noise]."
   "Then you put two of the bamboo . . ."
   "The audience love the performance and enjoyed them self."
   "Two or three time."

Absence of pluralization was very common in students' writing.

6. Inadequate use of SJE rules

When the Jamaican tries to move along the speech continuum, he or she dispenses with some Jamaican Creole rules and tries to adopt SJE rules, such as verb inflection. However, this may be done inconsistently or improperly.

The following are examples of the misapplication of the rule of inflection:

"An then we heard the horn starts to blow."
"To fixed . . ."
"The children needs to have behaviour."
"Then you mixed it with a spoon."

They may use the wrong inflectional ending, e.g.
"The [sic] started given the beat."

Or they may pluralize inappropriately, e.g.
"The peoples."
"If the drinks is fresh."

7. Inconsistent use of tense markers

This problem may be another form of that discussed in 5 above. Teachers referred to this as tense shifting or mixing of tenses. Most students shifted from one tense to another, e.g.

"And then the thing that we were waiting for at the beach, we play games and swimming a lot."
"Then you would stir it and minced up the peas."

8. Use of Creole words and phrases

As discussed earlier, Jamaican Creole differs from SJE not only in syntax but in vocabulary as well. It uses SJE words in contexts and with meanings not usually found in SJE. As Roberts (1988) observes, "Creole English has a number of basic words each of which covers a greater semantic area than the same word does in Standard English" (p. 79). Students revealed this tendency in their writing, and in general showed that they had a very limited vocabulary. The following are examples of this use of Creole words and phrases:

"You throw some salt in the peas."
"Children have no behaviour to no teacher."
"I saw lot of places and things like for instant the houses."

9. Absence of the auxiliary "be" to express continuous action

This problem occurred less frequently than those discussed above. The auxiliary was omitted for both the present and the past, e.g. "me going".

10. Use of an adjective to express action

This was also a less frequently occurring problem. Roberts (1988) refers to this use of the adjective as the adjectival predicate; it represents Jamaican Creole's tendency to use SJE words in a broader context than in SJE. Thus students wrote sentences such as:
"The tail will heavy down the kite."

These ten writing problems are a result of Creole interference. In addition, students displayed other major writing difficulties including
• poor sentence structure or syntax,
• incorrect spelling,
• lack of knowledge of the mechanics of writing,
• a limited vocabulary,
and even in some instances, an inability to understand instructions. Examples of the first four difficulties are given below.

11. Poor sentence structure or syntax

Most students were unable to write correct compound sentences. One reason may be that they are unaccustomed to using relative pronouns which are almost non-existent in Jamaican Creole, or to link correctly subordinate and main clauses. Examples of compound sentences were:
"So that the children can have some ware [sic] to play and don"t play in the street so the cars can drive."
"I don't now [sic] if the teachers are comfortable on there [sic] seat and the floor its [sic] too dirty that's why I think it need carpet."
"Any teacher hear you it would be sorry."

121

12. Incorrect spelling

Virtually all students made many spelling errors — even of simple words such as curse (cruse), with (whith), next (nexed). Much of this problem is attributable to the influence of Creole pronunciation. Thus, students wrote:

nize (noise)	by (buy)
masqueeta (mosquito)	had (add)
rang (wrong)	seirous (serious)
affer (after)	gard (guard)
of to (have to)	some ware (somewhere)
elsha (Hellshire)	raffel (raffle)

13. Lack of the mechanics of grammar and writing

Included in this heading are the following:
- Use of the wrong prepositions: e.g., "into" for "in". Examples are "squeeze some lime inside it"; "lower the prices off some goods".
- Use of the double comparative: e.g., more harder, more nicer, more better
- Use of the wrong pronoun e.g., "who" for "which" or of an adjective as a pronoun: "People can't feel comfortable were their are."
- Omission of the definite or indefinite article: e.g., "It need carpet."
- Lack of punctuation
- Inappropriate use of capital letters

14. Limited vocabulary

Students used the same (often simple) words repeatedly throughout their writing. They often used words inappropriately, in addition to spelling them incorrectly. These two problems can be attributed to their limited vocabulary.

These major problems — some resulting from Creole interference, others a result of inadequate instruction or practice in writing, were detected in the pre-test. They also recurred in students' diaries. Of the 240 students, roughly 15 to 20 wrote essays which were free of the above problems or which had only a few spelling errors.

Students' reading

The diagnostic Reading Test was administered to the students over a six-month period. The Reading Test or Informal Reading Inventory (Dilner and Olson, 1977) consists of a series of passages written at different grade levels. In this test, Level 1 is equivalent to Grade 1, level 2 to Grade 2, and so on. The results of the reading test showed that only 24.1 percent of the students in Grade 7 were reading at the level of Grade 4 or above. Seventy-six percent were reading below the level of Grade 4.

Students' engagement in the activities

Term 1 – Speaking

The main purpose of the teaching/learning activities in the first term was to encourage students to speak, to express ideas to an audience, and to develop some confidence in themselves as English speakers. The topics drew on the students' immediate and personal experience, e.g., the Common Entrance Examination, leaving one's old school, expectations for high school, and feelings about self and others. In all the classes, students were initially very shy to speak and even to work in groups. But after the initial sessions, nearly all students entered into these discussions with relish, eager to have their ideas heard. Extracts from field notes of these lessons read as follows:

Almost all students appear interested and are listening to the presentation.

Students appear attentive and obviously want to contribute.

This interest in the topic under discussion is borne out in the entries in journals made by many students. As one student wrote: "This kind of English teaches me a lot of things and it makes English interesting." The assignments elicited students' written and spoken language. Interviewing each other or interviewing members of the community, and class presentations required conferring among group members, organizing their thoughts, writing, and later speaking in class. Important cognitive processes were involved, for example, listening to and evaluating presentations, making inferences about motive and character in the discussion of a poem, and doing creative

123

writing (e.g., a poem, a play). The assignments also gave teachers the unusual opportunity to find out more about students. Teachers reported that they discovered that some students are intelligent, thoughtful, and knowledgeable, and that they gain much information from television. These discussions allowed students to bring their experiences, ideas, and concerns to the teaching/learning encounter.

During this first term, the many assignments gave students ample opportunity to use SJE, or to speak closer to the SJE end of the language continuum. But unprepared spontaneous discussions were often in Jamaican Creole. In one instance, a student tried to present her views in SJE, failed and asked to speak in Jamaican Creole. And students found it difficult to do a dramatization in SJE. In classroom assignments, students' limited vocabulary became evident.

There were marked differences in teaching style, which potentially could lead to differences in student learning. One teacher questioned, explained, probed, elaborated on points, while the other for the most part accepted students' responses often without comment. There were also differences in the method or style of classroom management. These differences may explain in part the difficulties of classroom management experienced by one teacher.

In addition to their knowledge and experiences, students brought attitudes and behaviours which at times worked against the goals of the teacher. Some boys, particularly those in one of these two classes, observed, mimicked, teased and joked at the slightest opportunity – obviously not taking the task seriously. For example, when the word "hypocrite" was used during one lesson, some boys began to coin words to rhyme with it: "micorite", "ticorit", chuckling and laughing among themselves. There was evident, at least in this class, a distinct male student culture which conflicted with the goals of the group. One female student (who was exceptional in her writing ability) expressed her frustration with this behaviour in her journal:

"I don't know why I had to come to this class with these children. We're going to get into more trouble (Jan/90). Most of the trouble makers in my class are boys and one or two are girls (April/90)."

Despite the inherent interest of the topics, and the positive response of the students, the instructional method used in these activities prevented the lessons from being fully effective. The method of whole-group instruction contradicted the intent of these activities which was to give students a chance to express themselves and to develop confidence in doing so. The whole-group instruction meant that only one student could contribute at any time. Since all or most were eager to present their ideas, many students became frustrated. Very often individuals – and not only those at the back of the room – began to chatter or mutter or murmur, after they (again) had not been given a turn. At some points in some lessons, the participation rate was roughly 30 percent. In the two classes observed during the first term, effort was rarely made to regain the attention of students who were engaged in private chatter.

Towards the end of the first term, students had the opportunity to express their views on the new curriculum. They referred primarily to the new approaches which were different, varied, and interesting, and which allowed them to express their ideas. They contrasted these approaches with the traditional approach which was seen as teacher-directed and uninteresting. Teachers also felt that students enjoyed these activities, which provided much opportunity for language use. They commented on the willingness of students to speak in front of others, and the self-confidence which they now displayed. They also referred to the increased receptivity to the use of SJE. In two classes, it was found that one or two students who always spoke SJE were now listened to with respect. By the end of the term, therefore, there were positive reactions to the programme. The only reservations related to the absence of writing exercises. Teachers reported that some students wondered aloud when they would begin to write. Some parents also felt that something was lacking from the curriculum.

Term 2– Writing and Speaking

The second term was devoted to Unit 1 – Our Language. The activities were designed to encourage students' expression of ideas in speaking, writing, and reading. For example, after reading, discussing and dramatizing the story of "Androcles and the Lion", students were asked to write a story of an occasion when they showed kindness or were shown kindness.

From the very beginning, teachers adopted the practice of choosing the worst script or one with many glaring errors, and allowing students to correct the errors. Thus, students had the opportunity to think about the language they use, to develop a critical attitude and a

125

sensitivity to correct usage. They also of course learned the correct SJE forms of Jamaican Creole. Much time was devoted to the expression of past time in SJE, and to punctuation. Examples of class activities are presented below to illustrate how these activities helped students to learn not only facility with SJE but other cognitive skills as well as self-confidence.

Students soon learned to pick up errors of grammar and syntax as well as punctuation. At the same time, they became aware of the importance of self-confidence and voice projection in speaking. In the follow-up lesson to the story about "Androcles and the Lion", which I observed three weeks after the beginning of term, a student made the following presentation:

"One morning when I was going to school, my mother gave me $1.50.

I was walking and I saw a man begging money. The only money I had I gave to him. He was glad. One day I found $50.00. I was over excited. I was in school and I went home. I saw a box and inside was a mongrel and from that day we were friends."

The student spoke without a script. He spoke almost perfect SJE, though his diction seemed uneven. Thus after three weeks and with some preparation, this student (who normally spoke Jamaican Creole in conversations with his friends) was showing some facility in moving along the speech continuum.

Students, however, had been listening and were quick to point out some errors of pronunciation:

"He said one mawning."
"He said my modder."
"He was nervous, miss."

Thus, it was not only the student who prepared and made the presentation who benefited. The other students were developing their ability to listen and critique what is heard and thus improve their language ability.

One feature of the alternative approach to teaching adopted in this curriculum was the opportunity for students to examine their own work or the work of a fellow student, to examine the grammar or mechanics of the writing, and to think of or reason through the correct form to be used. In this process, students considered the intention of the writer, and the context in which a form is used. The following is an example of this process taken from field notes dated February 19, 1990. Students have been presented with an extract of the description of a good deed. There are few punctuation marks. The teacher begins by discussing quotation marks and when each is used. By allowing students to comment on the use or appropriateness of certain quotation marks in particular sentences, the teacher learned what students thought about the topic and thus was able to address their misunderstandings.

This is illustrated in the following exchange:

Teacher:	*"Now someone said you can use the exclamation mark with Help Help."*
She writes:	*"Help! The house is on fire."*
Some students suggest:	*"The close quotation mark should be placed at Help."*
Others suggest:	*"It should be placed after fire."*

Ian suggests that we have to put a comma after the exclamation mark.

Teacher:	*"It is like a question mark. You don't put a comma after the question mark, do you?"*
Teacher writes:	*"Help! The house is on fire, cried the boy."*
A girl reads:	*"Help [pause] the house is on fire"* and suggests that we should put the quotation mark after help, because there's a pause.

The teacher explained that the exclamation mark suggests a pause, thus a comma is not required.

This discussion illustrates one of the advantages of the alternative approach. The teacher discovers what the students think and is thus able to clarify misconceptions which she would otherwise not know existed. In this same lesson the class continued to examine the poorly written work of one or two students. The activity in this lesson also allowed them to think about intention, expression and meaning within a passage:

The teacher begins:	*"Now we're going to look at the story and read the first sentence."*
Student:	*"I don't know what's the first sentence 'cause there's no full stop."*
Teacher:	*"Okay. Let's see if you can construct something from the first few lines."*

127

Student reads and then interprets what is written.

Student:	*"The 'when' don't sound good there."*
Teacher:	*"When don't sound good?"*
Student reads, changing the written work:	*"One day my mother told me to go to the shop to buy a pack of butter for her."*
Student:	*" 'For her' is not necessary because we know it's her mother."*

Another student suggests we use purchase instead of buy.
Another student suggests that if he is to buy, we know that he is going to the shop, so to the shop can be omitted.

Another student reads:	*"Last week Saturday my mother sent me to buy a pack of butter at the shop."*
Teacher:	*"Is it saying the same thing?"*

The class continued to discuss phrases used in the student's work, and the points where punctuation is needed to mark off complete thoughts.

In this extract, from a lesson observed on February 19, 1990, students examined their own writing about their own experience, analysed it, and suggested alternative and better ways of expressing the ideas. By doing this, they not only learned how to express their thoughts in SJE, but they developed a critical attitude and a disposition to think about the quality of their written and spoken work. Students had by the time this lesson was observed, had ample opportunity to be not only aware of wrong structures and phrases in SJE, but the correct SJE forms. The teachers were allowed some flexibility in extending the curriculum to suit the students' needs and the teacher's own assessment of what was necessary. Most had decided to give students some drill exercises in areas such as concord in the present tense and use of the past tense. Such drill exercises supplemented the alternative approach.

We have already seen that the alternative approach allowed the students the opportunity to listen carefully to class presentations in order to detect errors and to make judgments about quality. They also, as seen in the above examples, thought about and analysed language. The activities also required students to engage in other cognitive processes. For example, students engaged in problem-solving, determining and expressing their personal reaction to a poem, and explaining why a verse was more appealing than another. In one activity in which students had to dramatize a story, they were asked to prepare a script, while being informed by the original story. And on many occasions, when students discussed poems or short stories, individuals were required to analyse character and plot as well as discuss the moral dimensions or the consequences of one's behaviour.

There were, however, some lessons which did not adopt the alternative approach to language teaching. Lessons devoted to Comprehension followed traditional patterns both in the design of the activity and in its execution. In such a lesson, the teacher typically had the students read the passage aloud once. She then asked questions based on the text to the entire class; students put up their hands and waited to be called upon. Because the teachers failed to adopt grouping, many students could easily become distracted and fail to participate. In the two Comprehension lessons observed, there was low participation at various points throughout the lesson; at such points the teacher rarely tried to engage the students' attention. In short, the traditional Comprehension lessons contradicted the principles of the programme, and for the most part lacked interest and student involvement.

The two teachers observed during the second term had the ability to establish a good, warm teacher/pupil relationship, to command respect, and to get students to pay attention to the task. One was especially encouraging of students' work. The other had a more authoritative (though not authoritarian) teacher presence. It was noted that in these two classes, problems with classroom management were kept to a minimum. In the atmosphere established by these teachers, students seemed more disciplined, participated more, and engaged frequently in class discussions. Hence, they learned more.

Though many students demonstrated that they were making progress in respect of self-confidence, recognizing errors, and even in their written presentations, many continued during the second term to use Jamaican Creole or to show evidence of the Creole influence in their speech. For example, in reading from written materials, students were heard to pronounce "were" as "was", "simply" as simple. They frequently dropped their "hs" and the "s" at the end of a word. And the lack of inflection (past and present tense) was also noticeable, as in "it don't done", "it finish". Students' vocabulary sometimes prevented them from expressing their thoughts. When asked during a comprehension lesson what "painful but necessary" meant, a student tried unsuccessfully to explain it in Jamaican Creole, saying finally, "never must, miss". This difficulty or inability to comprehend or express complex ideas was often observed in classrooms.

In their reflection on the term's work, teachers felt that the activities engendered interest and much participation. They referred especially to an activity in which students learned about animals and their communication. But two teachers complained that many students, mostly boys, were unwilling or unable to work effectively in groups even after a term of such experiences. Many students (about 40 percent) in two of the classes continued to believe that speaking SJE was a joke or an embarrassment. In addition, they continued to display severe problems in comprehending written material. One teacher stated that students often had ideas but could not express them in SJE. Nevertheless, they agreed that a climate had now been created where students were aware of the importance of Standard Jamaican English and frequently corrected others or accepted corrections from others.

Teachers reported again that they became more aware of students' wide knowledge, often picked up from television, less frequently from trips abroad or to the country. They agreed that the alternative approach to teaching made it easy for the teacher to learn about students and for the student to bring his own experience to the teaching/learning encounter. Teachers also remarked on the obvious contributions being made to the development of students' social skills. The act of interviewing others, forming and stating their own opinions, helped to make them more confident human beings.

Term 3 – An integrated project
This term was entirely devoted to the term assignment, a culmination of the unit on Communication. The assignment was:

- Divide the class into groups to research the communications advances made by the following groups and individuals: Egyptians, Phoenicians, Greeks, Gutenberg, Marconi, Bell
- Assign other groups to find out about the inventions of the telegraph, motion pictures, television, and the computer

- Organize a Communications History Parade in which students display their work

For each lesson, each class was divided into nine groups of four or five students and required to work together on the project. In the lessons observed during this term, the problems of group functioning which were evident in the previous terms, again surfaced. Nevertheless, this activity also provided excellent opportunities to use all language skills in an integrated project – reading, writing, speaking, discussing, sharing responsibilities, and planning. This final presentation was by reports, very impressive, at least to the teachers, as students displayed all the skills which they had learned over the year – confident self-expression, an improved ability to speak SJE.

Student outcomes

The outcomes of the project will be discussed in terms of students' writing, and personal changes detected in students' behaviour and attitudes.

Students' writing

Students' writing on the pre-test administered at the start of the project were analysed. The performance of each student on each test was then compared. Since the instructional emphasis during the year had been placed on the use of the tense marker "ed", this category of error was analysed in detail and will be reported here. The scripts of thirty-six students from all six Grade 7 classes were chosen for scrutiny. The changes in their performance with respect to the use of the past tense marker "ed" are presented in Table 2 below.

Table 2: PERCENTAGE OF STUDENTS WHO DEMONSTRATED CHANGES IN THE USE OF TENSE MARKERS ON TESTS

	No errors in pre-test and post-test	Decrease in proportion of errors made	No change or increase in proportion of errors made	Total
Number	3	13	26	36
Percentage	8.33%	36.11%	55.56%	100%

Table 2 shows that only among a significant minority of students — 36.1 percent — was there evidence that students had applied the principle of the use of tense markers to·express past time. Among these thirteen students most were able to use the tense marker consistently so that none of this type of error was detected in their post-test. A few students were inconsistent, though they clearly used the tense marker more frequently on the post-test. The majority of students in this sample, however (55.5 percent), ignored the use of the tense marker where it was appropriate. And for a small minority (8.3 percent), proficiency in the use of the tense marker was evident on the pre-test as well as on the post-test.

Punctuation was the second major problem which was emphasized in instruction. This was examined under the general category of sentence construction. This type of error was analysed without calculating proportions. By taking a comparative look at the results of both tests, it was obvious that no significant change had taken place in students' ability to determine when punctuation marks were needed to write compound sentences or to express complex ideas in a SJE sentence. Indeed there were more instances of poor structure on the post-test than on the pre-test because students wrote longer essays.

The difference in the length of the essays — particularly the ones related to the past and the future conditional — was commented on with some delight by both teachers and the students themselves. In many cases the assignments were double in length. Students obviously had more ideas and were not shy to express them.

A comparison with the control group of Grade 7 students at a comparable high school had to be limited to the post-test results only. For in the pre-test, only a few of these students wrote the essay which required the use of the past tense marker. Of the thirty-four students among the control group who wrote the past tense assignment, six or 17.5 percent made no past tense errors; 9 or 26.4 percent made one to two errors (which means they used the past tense inconsistently), and 19 or 55.5 percent consistently used the infinitive (or present) form of the verb to express the past tense. The problem of sentence structure and punctuation was present in nearly all essays in both pre-test and post-test.

Changes in students' writing as a result of the programme was also sought in students journals. During term two the programme focused on the most frequently occurring errors made by students.

Teachers chose the absence of tense markers and punctuation as the two most serious errors. By late January, students had begun to critique badly written pieces of work and to think through the correct forms of the verb and the punctuation marks which were needed. By late February and early March, a marked improvement in the use of tense markers was evident in many of the journals. Forty-two journals from three of the Grade 7 classes were then examined in depth to determine the nature and extent of the improvements made by students. The journals were coded into three categories: those in which tense markers and punctuation were used from the beginning of the year, those in which improvements in the use of tense markers and in punctuation were evident, and those in which no improvement was detected. The number and percentage of students in each category are presented in Table 3.

Table 3: PERCENTAGE OF STUDENTS WHO DEMONSTRATED CHANGE IN THE USE OF TENSE MARKERS AND PUNCTUATION IN JOURNALS

	Tense markers and punctuation good from the start	Changes evident in the use of tense markers and in punctuation	No change in the use of tense markers or punctuation	Total
Number	7	16	19	42
Percentage	16.7%	38.1%	45.2%	100%

Table 3 shows that of the forty-two journals, seven or 16.7 percent were, from the first entry, characterized by proper use of tense markers and punctuation marks. These students also had many ideas to express and wrote at length. They also demonstrated few of the other errors typical of the cohort. But these seven students all had difficulties with spelling, some to a greater extent than others. These spelling errors can be attributed to the influence of Creole pronunciation. It was not expected that these seven students would show any appreciable improvement in their journal entries. Another sixteen or 38.1 percent made marked but inconsistent improvement in the use of tense markers and punctuation marks after February. A few of these students also wrote longer pieces expressing more ideas as they became more accustomed to journal writing. Nineteen or 45.2

percent made no improvement in the use of tense markers or in the ability to write in sentences.

Those who showed some improvement in the use of tense markers and in punctuation showed some inconsistency in the application of these SJE rules. It appears that students in the process of learning to apply the rules do so on some occasions but not others. The following are three extracts from Mandy's journal (not her real name):

"Today we learn about some interesting about friendship and how we can help people and what is common about them and what is about them and the song we sing tell us about loving and that we must shear [sic] . . ." December 11, 1989

"When Miss came inside she asked what we got the last time and we told her, and she said that we are going to do communication then she asked what is the meaning . . ." April 5, 1990

"Today I enjoy myself doing English in my class. We learn about communication and she gave us some pictures. . ." April 9, 1990

The second passage illustrates the improvement evident in both punctuation and the use of the tense marker. But in the third passage, though she has now learned to write in sentences, the student reverts to omitting the tense marker "ed" on the verb.

It must be pointed out, however, that the only areas in which improvements were seen were the two areas on which teachers specifically focused and for which a special technique was adopted. The other major problem areas continued in the journals of most students.

Personal changes in students

Most Grade 7 students entered this high school lacking in self-confidence, reticent about speaking out in class or expressing their ideas in public, and ill at ease with the English language. A significant minority of students also considered that speaking SJE was laughable, almost embarrassing. By the end of the year, however, there were marked differences in the behaviour and attitudes of most students.

The increased self-confidence and willingness to speak and express ideas have already been discussed. We have also seen that students began to develop a critical attitude to the spoken language, and gave and accepted criticism without rancour. A change in attitudes to SJE was evident from the fact that in one class, one student who always spoke or tried to speak SJE, and who was initially ignored or laughed at, later became a respected member of the class, often called upon to do special activities. Significant changes in behaviour, sense of self and even self-esteem were also evident among certain girls – albeit a minority – who consistently tried to speak SJE, and who began to take special interest in their appearance. These remarkable changes may be attributable to these students' involvement in other special activities of the programme. But there was a definite link to their disposition (and ability) to speak SJE.

In summary, after one year of "Operation English", there were observable positive effects on the majority of students. Their improved social skills, a better sense of self, and a more healthy attitude to SJE, augured well for later learning and development. Their performance on the writing assignments cannot be regarded as disappointing when one considers that they were required to change patterns of their native language which they had spoken and heard spoken for ten or more years. Indeed, when this fact is taken into account, these results may be considered encouraging.

7

Gender in the School Setting

Research conducted in Jamaica and elsewhere shows that girls and boys have different socializing experiences in the home, where they are usually assigned different tasks and, as a consequence, learn different skills. Students and their relationship with academic work, their desire for learning, their aspirations, their willingness to apply themselves to complete academic work, are all formed and shaped by the home – the first socializing agent. There is some evidence that boys and girls may learn different orientations to school work and to learning and in this respect are influenced differently by the mother and the father (Connell et al., 1982). This differential gender socialization continues when the child goes to school, society's next most powerful socializing agency. Although boys and girls follow the same formal curriculum, there may be subtle differences in the messages that they pick up from that curriculum. For example, at the primary level, they may receive biased portrayals of men and women and boys and girls. Robinson (1995) found that in a sample of primary level readers used in Jamaican schools, men and boys were more frequently represented than women and girls, and boys were often represented in active play whereas girls were often seen in passive play. Furthermore, men were portrayed in a range of occupations such as managers, astronauts, sportsmen, musicians, while women in the few cases where they were portrayed as gainfully employed, were presented as helpers, nurses, and teachers. Such readers are a site for gender socialization for they help to shape students' attitudes toward oneself, to others, and to life in general (Robinson, 1995: 6).

136

What is the lived reality of boys and girls at school? Are their experiences more or less similar, or do they differ, and if so, along what dimensions? Recent research shows that these experiences differ significantly at both the primary and secondary levels. In a recent study (Evans, 1998), it was found that by the time students reach Grade 5, there is a marked difference in their behaviour, aptitude, and work habits. The majority of Grade 5 and 6 teachers interviewed in this study believed that girls consistently did better work, were more diligent and conscientious, and took their work more seriously. Teachers made comments such as the following:

> Girls take their work more seriously.
> Girls are more hardworking.
> The girls appear more serious.
> The boys like to play a lot.
> The boys don't pay attention.
> You always have to be behind the boys to get them to work.

These differences in attitude to school work may be a result of the different skills, habits, and dispositions which they learned at home or the different experiences that they have at school. At this age, there is also a noticeable difference in a crucial skill that has implications for success at school – reading. Girls are more able to read, spell, and communicate than boys. Ability to read has been identified as one very important developmental hurdle (Slavin, 1996). Without this ability, the student finds school punishing and unsatisfying. Because girls are more able to read than boys, they perform better academically than boys at the primary level.

These differences continue at the secondary level. Gender plays an important role in structuring the students' experience in the classroom. In the same study, it was found that the behaviour of boys and girls in the classroom differed significantly. This difference was structured mainly by the behaviour of the boys themselves. It appeared that boys, by their behaviour, socially constructed the learning environment and the perceptions that teachers and girls formed of them, of their competence and sense of responsibility. The research assistants who observed this behaviour noted that boys and not girls were likely to be out of their seats, to walk around and chat with other students, to engage in activities unrelated to the tasks assigned, to fidget, to move around and tease others, when the class was unsupervised. Some of this behaviour was even observed while the teacher was present. Boys were also likely to absent themselves from devotion or from lessons, and to be seen strolling around the school while classes were in session. Such behaviour on the part of the boys was in stark contrast with that of the girls who were usually described as conforming, doing their work, participating, or sitting quietly.

Boys' behaviour, in turn, influenced teacher/student interaction, as well as teachers' and girls' reaction to boys. For example, teachers in this study thought that secondary boys were lazy or lacked interest in academic work or were less competent that girls. Consequently, they tended to pay more attention to and interact more with girls or they tried to encourage and motivate the boys. These differences in teacher/student interaction did not escape the notice of students. In the interviews with students, both males and females acknowledged that teachers treated boys and girls differently. Both boys and girls admitted that boys received more harsh and unfair treatment than girls. And they made a distinction between interactions where the focus was on instruction and those where the focus was on behaviour. In both cases, both boys and girls believed that the boys were unfairly treated.

The study also found that boys are more likely to receive corporal punishment and insults from teachers than girls. In the study just cited, 18 percent of boys compared with 10 percent of girls reported receiving corporal punishment in school. Approximately 30 percent of boys compared with 20 percent of girls said they did not like the way teachers treated them. Thus, both boys and girls experienced negative school practices and treatment at school, but boys were likely to experience more than girls. Boys were more likely to be found in the low stream than girls and low stream boys were more likely to be beaten and insulted than any other group of students. Other research supports the conclusion that in Jamaican schools girls are more likely than boys to like school, to be given more positive evaluations and have positive interactions with the teacher, to be seen as more well behaved, and be given more responsibility in the classroom (Keith, 1976; Evans, 1988, 1991; Parry, 1995). But there are subtle interactions among these characteristics. Colour, class, and ability may interact in many ways. For example, students from poorer backgrounds receive mainly negative evaluations and interactions, but their ability may have an influence on the severity of such interactions. Those from privileged backgrounds and those who are brown-skinned received both positive and negative evaluations, with academic ability and attitudes to the teacher being mediating factors (Keith, 1976).

We also know that there are differences in the academic achievement of boys and girls at all levels of the education system. Although more females than males enter for the regional examinations such as CXC, because there are more girls than boys enrolled at Grade 11, their performance is more or less equal, with females doing better in some subjects, and males doing better in others, and with their perfomance more or less equal in some (CXC Statistics, 1998).

In an earlier extract from research carried out by Yusuf-Khalil (1993), we learned of the experiences of low stream students in three primary and all-age rural schools. We saw that low stream students receive more negative evaluations from teachers and other students, are unfavourably compared with high stream students, and complain of severe corporal punishment. The extract below illustrates the gender differences in the experiences and perceptions of low stream students.

Girl in 6C:	*"The boys get beating every day, sometimes dem don't deserve it."*
Boys in a "C" stream:	*"She prefer the girls."*
	"The girls are brighter than the boys – teacher prefer the brighter children."
Girls in a "C" stream:	*"Boys get more beating – because they give more trouble."*

Boys agreed that they get more beating and that they were beaten more severely but disagreed with the reason which the girls gave. They believed that the teacher preferred the girls because they (the teacher and the girls) are both females. This sentiment was expressed by students in the high and low streams, as seen in the following comment:

Boy:	*"If fighting between boy and girl – boy get the beating. Teacher sey wi must not beat we wives, so she beat we if we fight the girls."*

Consequently, boys tended to be very condescending to the girls. "Tru yu a girl we don't lick yu back" (speaking to the girls).

Observations indicate that the more authoritarian the teacher, the more passive the girls appeared to be and the more aggressive the boys. As a result the following pattern emerged: The 6C classes consisted mostly of boys. In these classes, the boys were assertive and tended to take control of classroom activities; the girls tended to participate less. However, the girls could easily become assertive, even aggressive, if annoyed by the boys. The 6A classes consisted mostly of girls. In these classes, the girls were assertive and dominant during teaching/learning activities. The boys, on the other hand, participated less than the girls. In the "C" streams and the lowest group in the mixed-ability classroom, boys were in the majority and were usually regarded as "giving the most trouble".

In coping with the daily experience of schooling, low achieving girls usually conducted themselves in a quiet way. They sulked or cried when beaten by the teacher but retaliated if hit by a fellow student. These girls expressed a reluctance, even fear, of asking questions:

Girl: *"We don't question her – we afraid of her shaming us; she shout too much."*

Boy: *"When the girls don't buy the canteen food she sey dem betta mine dem belly"* [i.e. get pregnant].

Girl: *"Talk bout man dem a gi we lunch"* [in a hurt tone of voice].

In some cases girls try to protect their self-esteem by taking pride in personal appearance. But a girl's attention to her physical appearance can incur the irritation of some teachers, as seen in the comments of this teacher of Grade 6C.

6C – Teacher: *"See yu, yu just big and fat and lazy. Don't come back here tomorrow with those hairstyle. Plait your hair and put in your clips . . . You come here with hairstyle and don't put anything in your head."* (Speaking to a group of girls.)

Boys are equally subjected to verbal abuse but react more angrily than the girls.

Girl: *"She love shame the boys!"*

Boys: *"She call wi wanga gut – an say wi a thief."*

Researcher: *"How does the treatment make you feel?"*

Boys: *"Mek we behave wickeder."*

Girls: *"Mek we feel bad."*

Clive: *"Sometime the male teacher hit us with board."*

Researcher: *"What do you do?"*

Clive: *"Feel like lick him dung!"*

Researcher: *"Why don't you?"*
Responses: *"A don't want to get bad report."*
              "Want to learn" [feels he'll be sent from the school].
              "I am a little child, I wouldn't do that."

Boys and girls tended to be equally critical of teachers. If students did not like the teachers, they were prone to exaggerate – "jus looking at my teacher yu frighten" (indicating that she is ugly). But if they liked a teacher, they would bring small gifts of fruit and place it on the table. They also tried to think of ways to spite the teacher. This included doing things to annoy them and refusing to give them gifts on Teachers' Day. Students confided that it gave them a sense of pleasure and satisfaction to do so. These were not the only means of coping, however. During the period of investigation in the field, I was left with an impression of a level of deception that I had not previously credited students of this age capable of engaging in. Some students, it appeared, had successfully learnt how to "make-up" to the teacher, in order to avoid their punitive environment.

In this extract we see through the eyes of these students that boys are subjected to harsher treatment than girls, and that (female) teachers show preferential treatment toward girls. We also get a glimpse of the way in which the boys' attitude and resentment toward the girls is constructed within the school setting, and the close connection between their masculinity and corporal punishment. We also see the influence of the stream (high, medium, low or mixed ability) as well as gender on the peer culture that develops in a particular class. And we see from this case study the construction of a particular femininity – the fearful and passive female who is made to feel ashamed because of her physical appearance. And there is evidence that shame and humiliation are used to control students. This method of controlling students has different effects on boys and girls. It would appear that in circumstances such as the one described, boys are prone to anger and aggression and may even be tempted to be violent. The girls, on the other hand, express hurt and resentment.

The school is a very important site for the formation of personality and identity. And an important aspect of that identity is one's masculinity and femininity. The interactions that girls and boys have with each other and with the teacher, the valuations that they come to make of themselves as girls or boys, the attributions or inferences that boys or girls make about

141

causes and consequences of their behaviour as boys or girls – all serve to form their masculinity or femininity. This refers to the meanings that boys or girls develop over time about themselves, the ways in which boys and girls see and define themselves, and the kinds of behaviour that each accepts as appropriate for his or her sex (influenced of course by what society considers appropriate for each). These conceptions of self begin in the home and continue and are reinforced in the school. This gender identity – masculinity or femininity – is formed through social interactions, the kinds of reactions and responses one gets from teachers and peers. The development of gender identity is inescapable since each of us is either a female or a male. Unfortunately, this identity can also be tinged with certain affects such as shame, guilt, inferiority, superiority, condescension to the other sex and even feelings of aggression, as the extract above illustrates. The episode illustrates not only the circumstances under which girls and boys develop their notions of what it means to be boy or girl but the affects or emotions with which it is associated.

8

Toward Better Schools for All

The book began with a vision of what schools can aim for, the different outcomes that schools can hold out for its students. These aims are based on what some philosophers have articulated as the possibilities for education of the young, and as such, represent ideals. But schooling – the pursuit of education within an institutional setting – is always historically, socially, and culturally situated and, as such, inevitably constrains the achievement of our aims and ideals. There is thus the promise and the reality of education and schooling. Education holds out the promise of emancipation, of knowledge that can make one think and imagine, of understandings that can offer options and possibilities for young people, and alternatives to traditional ways of life and to localized knowledge and beliefs. But what is evident from the research reported in this book is that schooling, while holding out these possibilities also serve as a "contradictory resource" (Levinson and Holland, 1997). Though education and schooling are considered an important avenue for socializing the young and for inducting them into knowledge and disciplines that have currency in wider spheres, they also widen social class differences and academic abilities and lower self-esteem at least among some students. Schooling can therefore serve to bind many young people to existing possibilities based on class and to a lesser degree on colour and gender. Schooling holds out promises for all its students, but enables their achievement for only some. While I do not agree that the school and the state do this intentionally, as the social reproductionists would argue, there are mechanisms within the school and in the educational system itself that contribute to these differential outcomes. These mechanisms relate to aspects of structure and the processes in the school.

An important aspect of structure is streaming which, as we saw, is intricately connected to the competitive academic curriculum. Streaming sorts students into categories according to the students' knowledge of aspects of the competitive curriculum – knowledge that reflects the existing social structure and social and economic opportunities. Once students are categorized and streamed, they are likely to remain in that stream for the major part of their school career. Students remain in the low stream because of the initial gaps in their knowledge, the failure of many schools to address those gaps by means of meaningful remedial work, and the absence of teaching methods to accommodate different learning styles. But they remain there because they rarely get the encouragement, motivation or opportunities to do better. They are not expected to do better. And the attitudes of teachers and peers and the very nature of teacher/student interaction rob them of this motivation, a sense of empowerment and self-esteem. Streaming as a major aspect of school structure has a significant and long-lasting effect on students' access to knowledge and achievement, their self-esteem, aspirations for the future, the formation of social categories, and relations with other students. It serves to bind many students to their social class origins and to withhold from these students the emancipatory promises of education.

When the dominant aim of education and schooling is the passing of examinations, teachers and students tend to emphasize preparation for the examination; schools emphasize streaming and teachers use primarily the methods of lecturing and note-giving. All of this distorts the educational process, making educators lose sight of the laudable goals articulated by the MOEC. This process also ignores many important aims of education related to student development, and leaves behind a sizeable proportion of students.[1] Those students who need more attention, encouragement, and resources than the average or high ability students to make the grade very often receive less.

The ROSE programme which has now been instituted at the Grades 7 to 9 levels of education advocates mixed ability grouping – a recommendation that would in principle minimize streaming at the secondary level. However, there is some evidence that teachers find it difficult to make the change to mixed ability grouping and integration because of the challenge that it poses and because of their beliefs about how schools are run and how one organizes for teaching (Evans, 1993). Such evidence suggests that many teachers may not find it easy to implement the new policy. Research from the United States also suggests that making the change to mixed ability teaching may meet resistance from parents as well, as studies on the process of de-tracking in the United States have shown (Oakes, 1992; Oakes et al.,1996). In the study carried out by these researchers, some parents complained that de-streaming deprived their children of that competitive edge or gave the same chance to all (Oakes et al.,1996). Such reaction on the part of parents illustrates the link between streaming and the competitive academic curriculum.

Although the general aims of education in Jamaica make mention of cultural, aesthetic, and spiritual awareness, commitment to moral principles, self-esteem and quality education, in reality schools focus on the passing of external and national examinations as a measure of their success. We saw that the knowledge tested in these examinations is derived, for the most part, from the disciplines taught at the higher levels of education. Much of this knowledge is normally transferred via the lecture method; students' mastery of the curriculum is then tested in order to determine who knows enough to be granted the credential. Yet, the vast majority of students are not able to reach the grade level in the educational system to take those examinations. The majority of students drop out of school or are forced to leave for a variety of reasons, some of which have to do with their inability to master the curriculum itself as well as to cope with the adversities of streaming. Of those who are able to get to Grade 11 where they can take these examinations, roughly one-half on average are successful.[2]

In recent years, the MOEC has made progress in diversifying the curriculum, especially at the secondary level. In all secondary schools, students can now take a combination of academic and vocational subjects. They can also take some technical subjects in combination with these subjects. Yet, to achieve the goals for the broad development of our students, we need to broaden even further what is offered in the curriculum. With the explosion in information now available through technology, we need to rethink what is essential knowledge. We must give more thought to the ways in which young people relate to the different kinds of knowledge, now, and in the future. And we must consider the ways in which we can help students to think and to problem solve while learning such knowledge. It is also important to reconsider the format in which the academic curriculum is made available at Grades 10 to 11. Some students will need this knowledge in the packages in which they are now presented – for further learning at the tertiary level. Others will find this knowledge more useful if it is integrated with the demands of everyday life and with the demands of the workplace.

Above all, we need to rethink our definition of the educated person, as Levinson and Holland (1996) suggest. There are alternative paths to becoming an educated person other than the mastery of the traditional academic curriculum. What is important is that our young people be prepared to live and function in the society in the first years of the twenty-first century. We have seen that the objectives of education in Jamaica emphasize literacy and numeracy, which are basic academic skills or tools for learning. These academic skills constitute only one type of literacy. Young people in today's world need a broad range of what Hickling-Hudson (1999: 22) refers to as "sociocultural competencies". These competencies include the academic, the technical, the humanist (i.e., self-reflective) and the political. This framework suggests that focusing on the academic skills is a narrow conceptualization of literacy broadly conceived. Gaining this broad range of literacies is especially critical for schools to aim for especially in a developing country where informal, non-formal, and continuing education is almost non-existent for the vast majority of our people.

There are many issues of burning concern to today's society; and intelligent understanding of such issues is now a necessity for all young people, if we want to have a well informed and educated citizenry. Examples of these topics and issues include: Understanding Oneself; Human and Legal Rights of Citizens; You and the Law; Being a Consumer/Consumer Protection/Consumer Awareness; Growing up/Adolescence; Resolving Conflicts; Parenting and Parents' Rights and Responsibilities; Current Social Issues Facing the Society; Learning from the Internet and from Technology; Understanding Popular Culture; and Entertainment and Culture. There are many others that teachers, students, and community members can identify. Such topics would contribute to the sociocultural competencies that Hickling-Hudson advocates. They can be taught and learned in an academically and intellectually engaging manner to all students in ways that encourage problem solving and creativity. Learning and mastering these topics can just as effectively contribute to making an educated person. In fact, they are becoming increasingly essential. Organizing and presenting them in different modes (for example, in modules) with a range of strategies would make this knowledge more accessible to a broader range of students. When a wider range of offerings is available, students will be able to combine choices from the traditional academic curriculum with these courses on issues/topics that are attuned to the needs and demands of today's world. What is clear from the research conducted by Brown is that some students are now contesting the traditional academic curriculum while critiquing the teacher's methods and lack of caring.

Another aspect of structure is the shortage of teaching/learning materials. We have seen in Chapter 4 that many schools attended by the poor are underresourced – lacking in teaching/learning materials, equipment, and students' textbooks. When such materials are not available, and in particular when students lack textbooks, it directly affects teaching practices. Teachers have to rely on other less effective methods such as writing on the chalkboard. We saw from the research extract that student disinterest and lack of involvement and ultimately their academic performance are not solely a result of student ability. They are socially constructed within the classroom setting and result in part from the lack of resources. Shortage of teaching/learning materials is particularly acute in the all-age, primary, junior high, and comprehensive high schools. The model of teaching which ignores student learning and pedagogical principles was influenced in part by the shortage of resources. This model of teaching is still quite common in many schools.

School processes include teacher/student interaction, discourse with students, and teaching methods. We have seen that poor and low stream students are more likely to be subject to stigmatizing, demeaning discourse, and corporal punishment. While in the past students were willing to tolerate such treatment because of the promise of economic rewards or because of close links between the school and the home or community, these conditions do not always exist. The traditional unwritten contract regarding the teacher/student relationship is now being penetrated by students' understandings of the relationship between schools and the economy. Schools can no longer make good on the promises of the benefits of education possible some decades ago. Many students understand this. At the same time, students recognize that some teachers are not able or willing to relate to them in a caring way. As a consequence, they are unwilling to give the usual respect and deference in the absence of teachers' respect. Under these circumstances, the traditional teacher authority is reduced. This is a new development of which teachers must be very cognizant. The teacher/student relationship can no longer be taken for granted.

147

By focusing on students' experiences and perspectives with a cultural production or a cultural studies perspective, I have been able to portray the experiences of some students who are disadvantaged in schools. But when we centre the individual, as these theoretical perspectives require, it is not so clear what is the role of theory, and how it can serve the educator. For with these perspectives, we move away from the promise of rationality, predictability, and control. Working with these perspectives raises new challenges for the educator who wants to be guided by principles. How does the cultural studies perspective help the teacher? How can education and schooling benefit from the knowledge of how individuals or different groups respond to educational practices? What do we do with the knowledge that teachers create and perpetuate inequality on the basis of the students' personal characteristics and place of residence, for example? How do we help teachers face the many dilemmas that they do on a continuing basis, many of which cannot be reconciled? The fact that individual schools and teachers structure inequality indicates that solutions rest in part with individual schools and teachers, though the state can have an influence by setting standards and creating incentives. It places a new responsibility on the educator to know and interact with students as individuals and to engage in teaching, with the knowledge that the teacher's power is awesome and that his or her impact is long-lasting and significant. It requires on the part of each teacher, more reflection on ends and means.

What some of the studies in this volume indicate is that much of this unequal and stigmatizing treatment is situationally constructed in classroom practices and specifically in the teacher/student relationship. We all have, to varying degrees, internalized the messages of a postcolonial society. Teachers are no exception. To change the practices which perpetuate inequality, lack of self-confidence and poor self-esteem on the part of students, requires a rethinking of the goals of education and a new role for the educator. We can learn from the example of Freire who educated illiterate peasants caught in a cycle of domination and oppression in a neocolonial situation in Brazil. Based on this work, Freire (1973, 1985) argues that education should be for critical consciousness, serving to transform attitudes and beliefs internalized under a colonial or postcolonial system. This transformation serves to "emancipate" and empower the learners. In this context, the educator has a significant role to play, but that role requires a critical attitude on the part of the teacher. It also requires a critical pedagogy. To be critical means that educators regard all aspects of the education act as problematic and subject to scrutiny. It requires that educators submit their work to systematic examination, bearing in mind certain facts and the possible consequences of one's behaviour (Carr and Kemmis, 1986). These facts could be the historical legacy of discrimination, the complexity of power relations in the classroom, and the potential for harm and for good which the teacher possesses. The teacher with this perspective bears in mind the social and historical context and constantly tries to avoid routine but discriminatory practices. He or she tries to engage in practices which are affirming especially for those students whose experiences make this very necessary. Critical pedagogy makes special demands on both the educator and the learners. The educator has to respect the learners, and the relationship has to be one of authentic dialogue (Freire, 1985).

Critical self-reflection and a critical pedagogy are essential in a postcolonial setting where there has been a denigration of black intelligence, black character, and black cultural forms. In the past, the school has at times been one of the agencies of this denigration. Today, the teacher has the power to arrest this denigration and move toward more democratic social relations in our schools and ultimately in our society. A critical approach to pedagogy represents a radically different approach to teaching and to the social relations within our schools. It would, above all, call into question the basis of the teacher/pupil relationship, the purpose of education and the experiences which can or should be accommodated in the curriculum. But it would also make educators more mindful of their role and the central role they can play in social change.

The human capital approach to education and development emphasizes the importance of the educated and skilled person to the development of nations. In Jamaica, this link between an educated populace and national development is seen in policy statements. For example, the 1990–95 Five-Year Plan was based on the "vision of the contribution which a refined education system is expected to make to the development of a creative, productive and caring society" (MOEC, 1991). But the qualities of caring, creativity and productivity, as well as those of discipline, problem solving, self-confidence and a sense of self, are formed in the socialization processes of the home and the school. If a large number of students experience schools where the processes required to develop and nurture such qualities are not in place, and where the development of the individual is not a central concern, these outcomes are not likely to be achieved.

149

Addressing inequality and the practices by which it is created is urgent in a postcolonial society which was founded on inequality, and which placed (and still places) more value on some cultural traditions, and social and racial/ethnic groups than on others. The legacy of this history is evident in the problems of identity, and a lack of self-confidence and self-acceptance among a significant number of children and young people in our schools and in the wider society. The existence of unequal and stigmatizing practices in a postcolonial society demands a radical reorientation and a new consciousness on the part of the school and of individual teachers. Since the 1960s, the MOEC has given priority to increasing access to education for a wider cross-section of Jamaicans, changing the curriculum to provide more quality education, and, in recent years, raising the level of achievement of students. Very little attention has been paid to the internal workings of schools and the processes by which and through which education is accomplished. The themes evident in the extracts from the research reported here indicate that urgent attention needs to be paid to such internal processes. These processes as well as the school differences in quality help to explain the paradox to which Gordon (1987) referred – that of large-scale social mobility coexisting with widening inequalities of opportunity. Only when such processes of schooling are changed can we hope to achieve the outcomes of productivity and creativity for all.

Notes

Chapter 1

1. In the early 1950s, access to a high school education was severely limited, with only about 1,250 students being admitted to high schools in 1952 (Miller, 1990: 214). These students were drawn mainly from the professional and highly skilled classes, with less than 2 percent coming from the unskilled and semiskilled groups. A major expansion of secondary education began in the 1960s with the construction of fifty junior secondary schools which were later upgraded to new secondary schools and are now being further upgraded to high schools and comprehensive schools. Since the 1960s, there have been other major educational reforms (see Miller, 1990 for a review), with the result that the number of secondary schools has increased dramatically, although there are still not enough secondary places to satisfy demand – especially at the upper secondary level. Although enrolment has increased, there is still some disparity in access to secondary education by the children from different social groups.

    The secondary high school is now attended by children from a wide cross-section of the society. But the children of the middle and upper middle classes are more likely to be represented in this type of school. For example, in the latest *Survey of Living Conditions* (PIOJ, 1998), the percentage of children from the different social groups attending high schools were as follows: quintile one (poorest) 20.3 percent, quintile two 23.4 percent, quintile three 28.6 percent, quintile four 36.4 percent and quintile five (wealthiest) 45.8 percent. The latest *Survey of Living Conditions* also shows that the comprehensive high school is also attended by children from all social classes though a smaller percentage (17.5 percent) of the population of these schools are from the wealthiest groups. By contrast, the all-age school, the new secondary school, and the primary and junior high schools are attended mainly by children of the poorer classes. The new secondary school is being phased out by the Ministry of Education and Culture and will become either comprehensive high schools or high schools.

2. The Reform of Secondary Education is a major innovation implemented by the Ministry of Education and Culture (MOEC) beginning in 1993. The first phase of this innovation focused on the Grades 7 to 9 levels; the second phase will address the upper secondary (Grades 10 and 11). ROSE aims at increasing access to secondary education, improving quality, and as a consequence increasing equality of educational opportunity. These aims will be realized by means of a revised common curriculum for all students in all types of school, as well as recommended teaching methods which are more activity-based. The new curriculum with its associated methods and materials, and its relevance to the society of the 1990s is expected to provide a quality education. It will also provide more balance between the traditionally academic curriculum and the demands of the workplace. Increased access to a secondary education will be achieved in large measure by the new curriculum, and in the case of the all-age school by the upgrading of Grades 7 to 9 section of this school. But

151

access will also be increased by the conversion of new secondary schools to comprehensive high schools and high schools (MOEC, 1993).

PEIP or the Primary Education Improvement Project aims at improving the quality of primary education by a revised curriculum that emphasizes problem solving. It employs a thematic approach to curriculum organization during Grades 1 to 3 and a subject centred curriculum organization at Grades 4 to 6. The curriculum replaces one that has been in operation since 1978.

3. Under the cost-sharing scheme established in 1994–95, parents are required to help pay the cost of their children's education. The government of Jamaica pays all school-level salaries, while parents contribute to the costs of teaching materials, books, supplies, utilities, maintenance, laboratories, sports and other facilities, and repairs. Each year, schools submit to the MOEC an estimated expenditure for the following year which is approved by the MOEC. This estimate reflects in part what the schools think the parents are able to pay, and determines the fees charged by the school. The fees vary widely by school type. For example, in 1998–99, the fees charged by the secondary high schools ranged from $3,500 to $8,100; fees charged by the comprehensive high schools ranged form $2,750 to $5,300. Over 70 percent of the comprehensive high schools charge less than $4,000 per year while 78 percent of the secondary high schools charge more than $6,000 (MOEC, 2000). Since these school fees are used in part to purchase instructional materials, some schools are at a distinct advantage with respect to providing quality education.

Parents who cannot afford to pay the fees are able to apply for exemption from the school fees under the Student Financial Assistance Programme. The all-age school and the primary and junior high schools, which are exempt from the cost-sharing programme, receive per capita subventions that are almost on par with the primary schools. In 1998–99, the per capita subvention to Grades 7 to 9 of these schools was $2,240 based on preliminary estimates (provided by the Statistics section of the MOEC).

Before the cost-sharing scheme was instituted, the MOEC allocated different subventions to the different types of schools. In 1987–88, the average per student subvention to the high school was $1,523.80, to the technical and vocational schools $2,765.60, to the new secondary school $1,216.80, to the comprehensive high school $1,134.40, and to the all-age school $581.10.

4. In 1994–95, there were 13,862 students in the Grade 9 of the all-age school and the primary and junior high schools. These Grade 9 students normally take the Grade Nine Achievement Test (GNAT) for entry to secondary schools and the Technical Entrance Examination for entry to technical high schools. However, in that year, only 9.8 percent of those taking the GNAT and 11.1 percent of those taking the Technical Examination were successful in gaining a place in a secondary school. These poor results are explained in part by the availability of places in these schools. Those students who fail to gain a place in a secondary school have little access to other types of secondary education. In the majority of cases, these students either return to the all-age or primary and junior high schools to repeat the examination or leave school.

Chapter 2

1. Having been borrowed from the Natural Sciences, these research methods were the prevailing orthodoxy in social research at the time that structural functionalism became influential in education. This orthodoxy – what became known as the "scientific method" – was borrowed by practitioners of the new discipline of sociology as the mode of enquiry most reliable in finding out about the individual and society. The scientific method requires the following: the "neutral" role of the researcher, interventions or experiments, controlled conditions during research, phenomena analysed into discrete variables and controlled for study, and a reliance on observation and instrumentation. Researchers who used these methods also adopted the principles of operationalism – a theory that defines scientific concepts in terms of the actual experimental procedures used to establish their applicability. This approach to research was termed positivist: a term used to describe the philosophy that the Natural Sciences provide a model for all inquiry, and that inquiry should rely only on what can be observed under controlled conditions. The positivists asserted that the aim of science is to establish general laws or to test their "truth".

   The disciplines of Sociology, Educational Sociology and Psychology – in particular Behaviourist Psychology – came to adopt this tradition of research, which has proved to be very influential in education (Carr and Kemmis, 1986). The theoretical framework of structural functionalism and its associated research methods acted as a conceptual guide for setting research questions. With an input-output model of education, the structural functionalists used the two most frequently used methods of research – the correlational and the experimental methods – to study the social inputs to education and the effectiveness of the school in carrying out its functions. The basic unit of analysis was some element of structure or a structure examined in relation to another structure (Bernstein, 1975). Research in this tradition is still the major type of research in educational sociology, as well as in other sub-fields of education. Correlational research aims at determining the relationships between and among variables. Experimental research is designed to identify interventions which may lead to improvements or desired outcomes.

Chapter 3

1. Many secondary school graduates choose to enrol in teachers' colleges because of the ease of entry, and relatively low fees and living expenses.
2. All names are pseudonyms.

Chapter 5

1. Although streaming by ability is the most prevalent form of grouping of students, others exist at the secondary level. Students may also be grouped according to the option (such as Science, Clerical, Arts) which they wish to

pursue. Such grouping, however, is not usually referred to as streaming. Sometimes, streaming by ability is practised within grouping by option. The MOEC has no official policy on streaming. However, the new ROSE curriculum for Grades 7 to 9 which is to be instituted in all secondary schools by 1999 advocates mixed-ability grouping.

Chapter 8

1. Based on the number of those assigned to the low stream in a recent study of secondary students with a sample of more than 3,700 students, it is estimated that roughly 25 percent of the students in our secondary schools are in the low stream. With roughly 220,000 enrolled at the secondary level in 1997 (MOEC Statistics, 1997), this translates to about 55,000 students enrolled in low stream classes at the secondary level in any given academic year.
2. In 1998–99, the following percentages of students passed these selected subjects in the CXC examination attaining Grades 1, 2 and 3 at the General Proficiency levels: Biology (51.5percent), Caribbean History (72.6 percent), Chemistry (41.4 percent), English Language (41.2 percent), English Literature (52.4 percent), Geography (67.7 percent), Mathematics (26.8 percent), Physics (38.2 percent), Social Studies (77.6 percent).

References

Anderson, P. 1997. *Youth unemployment in Jamaica*. Kingston, Jamaica: Department of Sociology and Social Work.

Anyon, J. 1981. "Social class and the hidden curriculum of work". *Journal of Education* 163: 67–92.

Apple, M. 1972. *Education and power*. Boston: Routledge and Kegan Paul.

Apple, M. 1996. "Power, meaning and identity: critical sociology of education in the United States". *British Journal of Sociology of Education* 17, no. 2: 125–44.

Ball, S. J., and I. Goodson. 1985. *Teachers' lives and careers*. Lewes, East Sussex: Falmer Press.

Becker, H. S. 1984. "Social class variations in the teacher-pupil relationship". In *Classrooms and staff rooms: The sociology of teachers and teaching*, edited by A. Hargreaves and P. Woods. Milton Keynes: Open University Press.

Bernstein, B. 1975. *Class, codes and control*. V.11. London: Routledge.

Bogdan, R. C., and S. K. Biklen. 1998. *Qualitative research for education*. Boston: Allyn and Bacon.

Bourdieu, P. 1977. "Cultural reproduction and social reproduction". In *Power and ideology in education*, edited by J. Karabel and A. Halsey. New York: Oxford University Press.

Bourdieu, P., and J-C. Passeron. 1977. *Reproduction in education, society and culture*. London: Sage Publications.

Bowles, H., and H. Gintis. 1976. *Schooling in capitalist America*. New York: Basic Books.

Brock, C., and N. K. Cammish. 1991. *Factors affecting female participation in education in six developing countries*. ODA Research Project 4532, Serial No. 9. Hull: Hull University.

Brown, D. 1994. *A Tracer Study of graduates of Jamaican secondary schools 1991–92*. Kingston, Jamaica: Education Research Centre.

Brown, M. 1992. "Caribbean first year teachers' reasons for choosing teaching as a career". *Journal of Education for Teaching* 18, no. 2: 185–95.

Brown, P. 1997. "Student behaviour and teacher-student relationship at a secondary high school for boys". Master's paper, Faculty of Education, University of the West Indies, Mona.

Bryan, B. 1998. "A comparison of approaches to the teaching of English in two socio-linguistic environments (Jamaica and London, UK)". PhD dissertation, University of London.

Caribbean Examinations Council. 1998, 1999. "Examinations statistics". Kingston, Jamaica. Mimeograph.

Carr, W., and S. Kemmis. 1986. *Becoming critical*. London: Falmer Press.

Cassidy, F. W. 1961. *Jamaica Talk: Three hundred years of the English Language in Jamaica*. Kingston, Jamaica: Institute of Jamaica.

Cicourel, A. V., and J. I. Kitsuse. 1977. "The school as a mechanism of social differentiation". In *Power and ideology in education*, edited by J. Karabel and A. Halsey. New York: Oxford University Press.

Coke, F. 1991. *Abandoning the chalkboard: An explanation of career change*.

Master's paper, Faculty of Education, University of the West Indies, Mona.

Coleman,. J. 1988. "Social capital in the creation of human capital". *American Journal of Sociology* 94: Supplement S95–S120.

Connell, R. W. 1985. *Teachers work.* Sydney, Australia: George Unwin.

Connell, R. W. 1996. "Teaching the boys: New research on masculinity, and gender strategies for schools". *Teachers College Record* 98, no. 2: 206–35.

Connell, R. W., et al. 1982. *Making the difference.* St Leonards, NSW, Australia: Allen and Unwin.

Craig, D. 1978. "The sociology of language learning and teaching in a creole situation". *Caribbean Journal of Education* 5, no. 3: 101–16.

Craig, D. 1981. "Language, society and education in the West Indies". *Caribbean Journal of Education* 7, no. 1: 1–17.

Darling-Hammond. 1995. "Inequality and access to knowledge". In *Handbook of research on multicultural education,* edited by J. Banks and C. Banks. New York: Macmillan.

Dei, G. 1995. "Drop out or push out? The dynamics of black students' disengagement from school". Paper presented at the annual meeting of the American Educational Research Association, 1995.

DeVos, G. 1992. *Social cohesion and alienation: Minorities in the US and Japan.* Boulder: Westview Press.

Dewey, J. 1916. *Democracy and education.* New York: Macmillan, Free Press.

Dilner, M., and J. Olson. 1977. *Personalizing reading instruction in middle junior and senior high schools.* New York: Macmillan.

Dreeben, R. 1970. *The nature of teaching: Schools and the work of teachers.* Glenview, IL: Scott, Foresman.

Erickson, F. W. 1986. ."Qualitative methods in research on teaching". In *Handbook of Research on Teaching, Third Edition,* edited by M. Wittrock. Chicago: Macmillan.

Erickson, F. W. 1987. "Transformation and school success: The politics and culture of educational achievement". *Anthropology and Education Quarterly* 18, no. 4: 334–56.

Erickson, F. W., and J. Shultz. 1992. "Students' experiences of the curriculum". In *Handbook of research on the curriculum,* edited by P. W. Jackson. New York: Macmillan.

Evans, H. L. 1988. "Reform of Secondary Education: General curriculum". Final report to the United Nations Development Programme and the Ministry of Education, Kingston, Jamaica.

Evans, H. L. 1991. "Teachers' and students' perceptions of teaching, learning and schooling in the all-age school". Final report to the Ministry of Education, Kingston, Jamaica.

Evans, H. L. 1993. "The choice of teaching as a career". *Social and Economic Studies* 42: 225–42.

Evans, H. L. 1994. "Review of policy relevant research on secondary education in Jamaica". Final report to Harvard Institute of International Education, Kingston, Jamaica.

Evans, H. L. 1998. *Gender and Achievement in Secondary Education in Jamaica.* Kingston, Jamaica: Planning Institute of Jamaica.

Feiman-Nemser, P. and R. Floden. 1986. "The cultures of teaching". In *Handbook of research on teaching*, Third Edition, edited by M. Wittrock. Chicago: Macmillan.

Figueroa, P., and G. Persaud. 1976. "Sociology, education and change". In *Sociology of education: A Caribbean reader*, edited by P. Figueroa and G. Persaud. Oxford: Oxford University Press.

Figueroa, P., and G. Persaud. 1976. *Sociology of education: A Caribbean reader*. Oxford: Oxford University Press.

Fine, M. 1986. "Why urban adolescents drop in and out of school". *Teachers College Record* 87, no. 3: 393–409.

Freire, P. 1973. *Education for critical consciousness*. New York: Seabury Press.

Freire, P. 1985. *The politics of education: Culture, power and liberation*. New York: Macmillan.

Giddens, A. 1979. *Central problems in social theory: Action, structure and contradiction in social analysis*. Berkeley: University of California Press.

Gilborn, D. 1998. "Young, black and failed by school; Education reform and black students". Paper presented at the annual meeting of the American Educational Research Association.

Goodlad, J. 1984. *A Place called school*. New York: McGraw-Hill.

Gordon, D. 1987. *Class, status and social mobility in Jamaica*. Kingston, Jamaica: Institute of Social and Economic Research Press.

Great Britain. 1901. Board of Education Report.

Greene, M. 1991. "Teaching: the question of personal reality". In *Staff development for the '90s: New demands, new realities, new perspectives*, edited by A. Liebermann and L. Miller. New York: Teachers' College Press.

Hall, S. 1996. 'Race, culture, and communications". In *What is cultural studies? A reader*, edited by J. Storey. New York: St Martin's Press.

Hamilton, M. 1991. "A review of educational research in Jamaica". In *Education and society in the Commonwealth Caribbean*, edited by E. Miller. Kingston, Jamaica: Institute of Social and Economic Research.

Hickling-Hudson, A. 1998. "When Marxist and post-modern theories won't do: The potential of postcolonial theory for educational analysis". *Discourse* 19, no. 3: 327–39.

Hickling-Hudson, A. 1999. "Experiments in political literacy: Caribbean women and feminist education". *Journal of Research and Development in Education* 3, no. 1: 19–44.

Jackson, P. W. 1968. *Life in classrooms*. New York: Holt, Rinehart, Winston.

Jackson, P. W. 1986. *The practice of teaching*. New York: Teachers' College Press.

Johnson, S. M. 1990. *Teachers at work: Achieving success in our schools*. New York: Basic Books.

Jones, A. 1989. "The cultural production of classroom practice". *British Journal of Sociology of Education* 10, no. 1: 19–31.

Karabel, J., and A. H. Halsey (eds.). 1977. *Power and ideology in education*. Oxford: Oxford University Press.

Keith, S. 1976. "Socialization in the Jamaican primary school: A study of teacher evaluation and student participation". In *Sociology of education: A Caribbean reader*, edited by P. M. E. Figueroa and G. Persaud. Oxford: Oxford University Press.

References

King, R. 1987. "The Jamaica Schools Commission and the development of secondary schooling". *Caribbean Journal of Education* 14, nos. 1 and 2: 88–109.

Levinson, B., and D. Holland. 1996. "The cultural production of the educated person". In *The cultural production of the educated person*, edited by B. Levinson, D. Foley and D. Holland. Albany: SUNY Press.

Lightfoot, S. 1983. "The lives of teachers". In *Handbook of Teaching and Policy*, edited by L. Shulman and G. Sykes. New York: Longman.

Lortie, D. 1975. *School teacher: A sociological study*. Chicago: University of Chicago Press.

Mac an Ghaill, M. 1994. *The making of men*. Buckingham, United Kingdom: Open University Press.

Martin, J. R. 1985. "Becoming educated: A journey of alienation or integration?" *Journal of Education* 167, no. 3: 71–84.

McDermott R. 1977. "Social relations as contexts for learning in school". *Harvard Educational Review* 47, no.2: 198–213.

McKenzie, H. 1986. "The educational experiences of Caribbean Women", *Social and Economic Studies* 35, no. 3: 65–106.

McLaughlin, H. J. 1994. "Looking back at myself: A soliloquy about classroom authority." *Teaching Education*, 6, no.1: 59–64.

McNeil, L. 1988. *Contradictions of control: School structure and school knowledge*. New York: Routledge, 1988.

Meeks, B. 1996. *Radical Caribbean: From Black Power to Abu Bakr*. Kingston, Jamaica: University of the West Indies Press.

Merton, R. 1968. *Social theory and social structure*. New York: Free Press.

Metz, M. 1978. *Classrooms and corridors: The crisis of authority in desegregated secondary schools*. Berkeley: University of California Press.

Metz, M. 1993. "Teacher's ultimate dependence on their students". In *Teachers' work: Individuals, colleagues and contexts*, edited by J. W. Little and M. W. McLaughlin. New York: Teachers' College Press.

Miller, E. 1990. *Jamaican society and high schooling*. Kingston, Jamaica: Institute of Social and Economic Research.

Miller, E. 1991. *Men at risk*. Kingston, Jamaica: Jamaica Publishing House.

Miller, E. 1997. *Jamaican primary education: A review of policy-relevant studies*. Kingston, Jamaica: Green Lizard Press.

Ministry of Education and Culture (MOEC). 1991. *Five-year development plan*. Kingston, Jamaica: Ministry of Education and Culture.

Ministry of Education and Culture (MOEC). 1993. "Reform of Secondary Education: A summary document". Kingston, Jamaica. Mimeograph.

Ministry of Education and Culture (MOEC). 1996. *Education statistics 1994–95*. Kingston, Jamaica: Ministry of Education and Culture.

Ministry of Education and Culture (MOEC). 1999a. "Education, the way forward: a green paper for the year 2000". Kingston, Jamaica. Mimeograph.

Ministry of Education and Culture (MOEC). 1999b *Revised primary curriculum grades 1–3, grade 4, grade 5, grade 6*. Kingston, Jamaica: Ministry of Education and Culture.

Ministry of Education and Culture (MOEC). 2000. "Cost sharing and school achievement". Kingston, Jamaica. Mimeograph.

Oakes, J. 1985. *Keeping track: How schools structure inequality.* New Haven, CT: Yale University Press.

Oakes, J. 1992. "Can tracking research inform practice? Technical, normative and political considerations". *Educational Researcher* 21, no. 4: 12–24.

Oakes, J., et al. 1996. "Change agentry and the quest for equity: Lessons from detracking schools". Graduate School of Education and Information Studies, University of California, Los Angeles. Mimeograph.

Okey, T. and P. Cusick. 1995. "Dropping out: Another side of the story." *Educational Administration Quarterly* 31, no. 2: 244–67.

Page, R. 1989. "The lower-track curriculum at a 'heavenly' high school: 'Cycles of prejudice' ". *Journal of Curriculum Studies* 21, no. 3: 197–222.

Pallas, A. 1993. "Schooling in the course of human lives: The social context of education and the transition to adulthood in industrial society". *Review of Educational Research* 63, no. 4: 409–47.

Parry, O. 1995. "Sex, gender and school failure". Paper presented at the Conference on Caribbean Culture, University of the West Indies, Mona.

Peters, R. S. 1967. "What is an educational process?" In *The concept of education,* edited by R. S. Peters. London: Routledge and Kegan Paul.

Piaget, J. 1968. *Structuralism.* London: Routledge and Kegan Paul.

Planning Institute of Jamaica. 1998. *Jamaica Survey of Living Conditions.* Kingston, Jamaica: Planning Institute of Jamaica/Statistical Institute of Jamaica.

Pollard, V. 1987. "Past-time expressions in Jamaican Creole: Implication of teaching creole". PhD dissertation, University of the West Indies, Mona.

Roberts, P. 1988. *West Indians and their language.* Cambridge: Cambridge University Press.

Robinson, E. 1995. "Examination of grade 6 readers to determine possible contribution to gender bias". BEd study, University of the West Indies, Mona.

Rose, M. 1989. *Lives on the boundary.* New York: Free Press.

Seaga, E. 1955. "Parent-teacher relationship in a Jamaican village". *Social and Economic Studies* 4, no. 3: 289–302.

Senior, O. 1991. *Working miracles: Women's lives in the English-speaking Caribbean.* London: James Currey.

Sewell, T. 1999. "Exploding the myth of the 'black macho' lad". In *Failing boys? Issues in gender and achievement,* edited by D. Epstein et al. Buckingham, United Kingdom: Open University Press.

Sikes, P. 1985. "The life cycle of the teacher". In *Teachers' lives and careers,* edited by S. Ball and I. Goodson. Lewes, East Sussex: Falmer Press.

Sistren. 1986. *Lionheart gal.* London: The Women's Press.

Slavin, R. 1990. "Achievement effects of ability grouping in secondary schools: A best evidence synthesis". *Review of Educational Research* 60: 471–99.

Slavin, R. 1993. "Ability grouping in the early grades: Achievement effects and alternatives". *The Elementary School Journal* 93, no. 5: 535–52.

Slavin, R. 1996. "We shall overcome: Key developmental hurdles to children's school success". Paper presented at the American Educational Research Association meeting, New York.

Solomon, P. R. 1988. "The creation of separatism: The lived culture of West Indian boys in a Toronto high school". Paper presented at the American Educational Research Association, New Orleans.

References

Solomon, P. R. 1992. *Black resistance in high school: Creating a separatist culture.* Albany: SUNY Press.

Stones, E. 1994. *Quality teaching: A sample of cases.* London: Routledge.

Stratton, J., and I. Ang. 1996. "On the impossibility of a global cultural studies". In *Stuart Hall: Critical dialogues*, edited by D. Morley and K-H. Chen. London: Routledge.

Tikly, L. 1998. *Postcolonialism and education.* Paper presented to the World Congress of Comparative Educational Societies conference, July 12–17, Cape Town, South Africa.

Turner, T. 1987. "The socialization intent in colonial Jamaican education". *Caribbean Journal of Education* 14, nos. 2 and 3: 54–87.

UNESCO. 1996. *What makes a good teacher? Children speak their minds.* Paris: UNESCO.

Wells, A. 1998. "Parent power". In *Education Life*, supplement of the *New York Times*. April 5.

Wexler, P. 1982. "Structure, text and subject: A critical sociology of school knowledge". In *Cultural and economic reproduction in education*, edited by M. Apple. Boston: Routledge and Kegan Paul.

Wexler, P. 1987. *Social analysis of education: After the new sociology.* London: Routledge and Kegan Paul.

Wilkinson, L. and C. Marrett. 1985. *Gender influences in classroom interaction.* New York: Academic Press.

Willis, P. 1978. *Learning to labour.* Westmead, England: Saxon House.

Yusuf-Khalil, Y. 1993. "What school is like for high and low achievers". Master's paper, Faculty of Education, University of the West Indies, Mona.

Index

Academic ability: dropouts and, 46–47; gender and, 22, 139; parents' decision making and, 47; self-esteem and, 46; streaming and, 49; teacher-student interaction and, 49; and teacher's response to students, 46

Authority: nature of, of teacher, 64; of the teacher, 50, 51–52

Boys: behaviour of, and teacher/student interaction, 138; and construction of learning environment, 137; corporal punishment and, 138; reading ability of, 137

Class: and parent-teacher communication, 48–49

Classroom interaction, 49; gender and, 137; importance of, 72

Classrooms: and learning, 14; physical context of, in all-age schools, 89

Collaborative learning principles, 68

Colour: and teacher's response to students, 48

Communication: between parents and teachers, 48

Competitive academic curriculum: and access to social resources, 70; features of, 70; and self-development of students, 72; and streaming, 145

Conflict model, 21; and cultural reproduction theory, 24; and educational practice, 22; examples of use of, in Jamaica, 22; and social reproduction theory, 21; weaknesses of, 23

Cooperation: in teacher-student relations, 54

Corporal punishment: in all-age schools, 88; boys and, 138; at Moonshine Primary, 95–97; reasons for applying, in all-age schools, 88–89

Cost-sharing scheme: explained, 152n. 3; in high schools, 12

Creole, Jamaican, 19, 105; differences between SJE and, 114–116; as language of instruction, 107; perceptions of, 105–106; structural differences between SJE and, 107; use of, in the classroom, 106–107

Cultural capital, 24

Cultural production approach, 26; and cultural studies, 18; and research on schools, 17–18, 148

Cultural reproduction theory: as conflict theory, 24; and school curriculum, 24; and schools, 24

Cultural studies: perspective of, and the teacher, 148; and postcolonial perspective, 18; and research on schools, 18, 148

Curriculum: academic, 69; and access to tertiary education, 70; competitive academic, 70; diversification of, 145; enactment of, 72; formal, 68; implicit, 71; integrated, 68; purpose of secondary academic, 69; subject-based, 68

Curriculum planning: in Jamaica, 68

Deception: by students, 141
Discipline: at Moonshine Primary School, 95–97; pedagogy and, 65; streaming and, 65
Dropouts: reasons for, 46–47
Dual system: of education in Jamaica, 19–20

Education: access to, in Jamaica, 3–4, 70, 151n. 1; of Caribbean women, 7; dual system of, in Jamaica, 19–20; goals of, 4–7; and life transitions, 8; objectives of Jamaican, 146; policy statements on, 5, 144; rethinking of goals of, 148; and social mobility, 2–4; tension between schooling and, 10
Education, tertiary: access to, 70
Educational experience: family background and, 47
Educational research: theoretical perspectives in, 25
Educational theories, 16–24; value of, ix
English language: CXC results in, 107; effectiveness of teaching methods, 107; role of, in educational system, 106;
Ethnographic research, 26
Examinations: CXC, 69; focus of schools on, 145; SSC, 69

Family: background of, and students' educational experience, 47; social capital of, 47–48

Garvey, Marcus, 24
Gender: and academic achievement, 22, 139; and classroom experiences, 137; corporal punishment and, 138; factors affecting socialization, 136; and peer culture, 141; and perceptions of low stream students, 139–140; in primary readers, 136; and schooling experience, 49; and streaming, 104, 138; and women in the workplace, 22

Girls: reading ability of, 137
Grade Nine Achievement Test (GNAT), 152n. 4
Green Paper on Education, 5

High achievers, 95; treatment of, by teachers, 102–103
Human capital approach: and national development, 149

Inequality: postcolonial studies and, 150
Inside Jamaican Schools: overview of, x–xii; purposes of, ix; research methods used, ix; theoretical perspective of, 27–29

Jamaica Union of Teachers (JUT), 22

Knowledge: rethinking of essential, 145

Language: what constitutes a, 106–107
Lessons: example of, in Language Arts, 80–86; example of successful, 74–80
Low achievers, 94–95, 154n. 1; and criticism of teachers, 141; effect of quality of instruction on, 97–98; effect of streaming on, 103; gender and perceptions in, 139–140; treatment of, by teachers, 102–103, 147

Mesolect, 106
Ministry of Education and Culture (MOEC) (Jamaica): and curriculum diversification, 145; and curriculum planning, 68; emphasis of, 150; Green Paper on Education, 5; policy statements on education, 5, 144
Mixed ability grouping, 94, 102; ROSE programme and, 144–145
Moonshine Primary: classroom atmosphere at, 95; discipline and punishment at, 95–97

National Vocational Qualification of Jamaica (NVQJ), 69

Operation English project: activities to

encourage speaking, 123–125; activities to encourage writing and speaking, 125–130; and administration of Reading Test, 123; assignment of integrated project, 130–131; data analysis in, 109–110; described, 108–135; effects of, 135; establishment of teaching/learning principles, 111; identification of problems of students, 110; outcomes of, 131–135; and personal changes in students, 134–135; research design and setting, 109; Rotary Club and, 108; students' attitudes to language, 113–114; students' competence in Creole and SJE, 114–116; teaching/learning activities, 112–113; writing ability of students involved in, 117–122

Parents: and communication with teachers, 48; and decision making relating to children, 47
Pedagogy, critical: described, 148–149; and teacher/student relations, 149
Peer culture: gender and 141; streaming and, 141
Postcolonial theory: cultural studies and, 19; described, 18; inequality and, 150; and the study of Jamaican schools, 19–20
Power: of the teacher, 52
Principals: role of, in schools, 14

Qualitative approaches: to educational research, 25–26

Race: and teacher's response to student, 48
Rastafarians, 24
Rewards: of Jamaican teachers, 33–34
Roles: conflict between teacher and student, 53
ROSE programme, 12, 151n. 2; curriculum of, 68, 71; and mixed ability grouping, 144–145
Rotary Club: and Operation English, 108

Schooling: as a contradictory resource, 143; differential benefits of, 9; gender and, 49; for high and low achievers, 94–102; and the human life cycle, 8–9; as a social activity, 6–7; and social mobility, 2–4; students and, x; tension between education and, 10; as unifying force, 8–9
Schools: approaches to the study of, 10; categories of, in Jamaica, 11, 13; ecology of, described, 13–14; and identity formation, 141–142; and personality formation, 141–142; in postemancipation Jamaica, 2; purpose of, 4; similarities of, 13; social informal side of, 7–8
Schools, all-age: attitudes to, 12–13; compared to high schools, 11; corporal punishment in, 88; lack of textbooks in, 87, 89; performance of Grade 9 students, 152n. 4; teacher/student ratio in, 73; teaching/learning in, studied 73–79, 80–86; teaching models used in, 74; upgrading of, 12
Schools, high: compared to all-age schools, 11; cost-sharing scheme and, 12; historical advantage of, 12; and social mobility, 11–12; and tertiary education, 12
Schools, secondary: types of, 13
Seatwork teaching, 80; consequences of, 87–88; features of, 86–87; use of time in, 86–87
Self-development: of students, and school curriculum, 71–72
Social capital: described, 47; and educational experience, 47
Social change: curriculum and, 65; role of the teacher and, 65
Social class: and teacher-student interaction, 48
Social reproduction theory: and conflict model of schooling, 21, 24; view of schools, 21–22
Social theory: task of, ix

Sociocultural competencies: described, 146–147

Sociology of Education: and structural-functionalist perspective, 21

Standard Jamaican English (SJE), 105; differences between Creole and, 114–116; structural differences between Jamaican Creole and, 107

Streaming, 9, 23; and academic ability, 49, 90–91; and access to knowledge and learning, 64–65; assumed advantages of, 91; benefits of, for teachers, 104; and competitive academic curriculum, 90, 145; described, 90; disadvantages of, 91–92; effect of, on low achievers, 103; effects of, 144; forms of, 153n. 1; and gender, 104, 138; in Jamaican schools, 91; and participation in school activities, 101–102; and peer culture, 141; and socioeconomic status, 94–95; and students' experiences at school, 92–93, 94; and students' self-evaluation, 98–101; and teachers' expectations and evaluations, 92; and tradition, 104

Structural-functionalism: assumptions of, 20; criticism of, 21; Sociology of Education and, 21; view of schools, 20–21

Students: academic ability and teacher's response to, 46; dependence of teachers on, for success, 54; educational experience and family background of, 47–49; evaluation and self-evaluation, 45; expectations of, at school, 7, 10; expectations of teachers, 49–50; influences on achievement and performance, 50; role of, 6; and schooling, x; self-development of, 71–72; views of school experience, 44–45

Teacher commitment: limits of, 43

Teacher-student relations, 6, 54; authority in, 50, 51–52, 57, 64; breakdown in, studied, 56–63; changes in, 147; cooperation in, 54; dominance and control in, 53; influence of boys in, 138; penetration of traditional, 147; power in, 52; school curriculum and, 72–73; social class and, 48; socioeconomic factors and, 138; and student' behaviour, 65; trust in, 65

Teachers: authoritarian, 95–96; burnout, 32; communication between parents and, 48; conflict, guilt and departure from the profession, 42–44; criticism of, by low stream students, 141; dependence on students for success, 54; example of positive characteristics, 79–80; function of, within the classroom, 51; identification with the profession, 43; initiation into the profession, 36–37; period of questioning and misgivings, 37–39; power of, 52; public attitudes to, 31; responsibility of, 54; role of, 6, 52–53; stages in deciding to leave the profession, described, 34–43; treatment of low stream students by, 102–103, 147, trust in, 65; and use of authority, 50–51; valuation and decision to leave, 39–42

Teachers' satisfaction: factors contributing to, 32–34

Teaching: approaches to, 6; characteristics of, 50–56; effect of quality of, on low achievers, 97–98; and enactment of curriculum, 72; seatwork model of, 80, 86–87, 88; stages in deciding to leave, described, 34–43; flat organization structure of, 33; rewards of, 33–34

Teaching/learning materials: and effective teaching, 73, 147

Textbooks: absence of, in all-age schools, 87, 89

Theoretical frameworks: purposes of, 16; relating to schools, 16–24

Tracking. See Streaming

Trust: in teacher-student relations, 65